# Harvest of Tears

by Alma Dettwiler

Cover Photo
Perry Murphy/Unicorn Stock Photos

Christian Light Publications, Inc.
Harrisonburg, Virginia 22801
1989

ISBN: 0-87813-530-8
Printed in U.S.A.

# CHAPTER 1

"It looks as if 1926 will be a good harvest year. Dad and I start cutting tomorrow. That means there will be money for me to go to college." John spoke happily, indicating the expanse of wheat past which they were strolling.

"You mean you haven't gotten over that idea!" declared Nancy.

"I wish you'd try to understand. I feel some-day God may call me to the ministry, and I need more Bible study. Whatever service God calls me into, I feel Bible study will be helpful. That's why I'm going to a Christian college."

"If I go to college, Marshall Bible College is the only place for me. I have enough faith that I have already enrolled."

"You have decided already?" Nancy asked sharply.

"Suppose it would hail?"

"Are you going to pray for hail?"

"Of course not. I wouldn't wish hail to destroy anyone's wheat crop and least of all your dad's. He's a wonderful minister." Nancy couldn't help thinking of John's dad.

Elmer Burns had been almost like a father to her since that bitter winter day he had called for her in the middle of the first grade arithmetic class.

She could still feel big Elmer tucking her into

the sleigh under the buffalo robe and hear him telling her that she no longer had an earthly father. "His place in heaven needed filling," he had told her. Now that she was older she thought only Elmer Burns could have said it so gently.

John's voice startled her. "You're doing some deep thinking. You haven't said a word the last mile."

"I was buried in the past. I was just thinking about your dad. I'll never forget how he came for me at school the day Daddy died. I knew my daddy was sick but didn't think about his dying."

"Pneumonia was serious in those days," John reflected. "And your daddy was overworked. He had just come back from holding evangelistic meetings somewhere, hadn't he?"

"Yes, he'd been to Nebraska for three weeks, and we were so glad he was home again." Nancy went on remembering. "Billy must have been three and he had been sick."

"Your mother has had to work hard all these years."

"Yes, but she always says she would not change it. God has ordered it this way. Mother is a great 'non-complainer.' She even thanks Him for the privilege of having had Daddy as long as she had."

"I hope someday God leads me to a companion like that. My folks say your mother's prayers and attitude were half of your daddy's success as a minister."

"John, do you really believe God leads you to a

6

companion?"

"Sure, if you ask Him for guidance."

"Your mother needs you at home when your dad is gone. Why must you insist on going away, John?" Nancy just couldn't leave the argument.

"Mom understands and wants me to go."

"But my daddy was a good minister and yours is too. Neither went hundreds of miles away to a college."

"I know." John started thoughtfully. "Dad says he never will have a way with the young people. Maybe if he'd have had more education—"

"That's silly. The young folks like your dad. Mother says Elmer Burns was accepted by everyone when he was ordained to take Daddy's place."

"Yes, well—I just feel God is leading me in this direction. Maybe you can come to Marshall after you graduate."

"That's impossible!"

"With God all things are possible."

"Anyway I don't care to go away and leave my mother just when I can earn money and make life easier for her." Nancy was angry because John did not say he would miss her. "You will soon forget me."

"I'll be home each summertime. I won't forget you. I waited a long time before your mother would consent to have me walk home with you Sunday evening after church."

Nancy knew it was true. Even though John was two years older than she, he had not dated, and Dry Forks boasted a lot of eligible girls. Her mother finally allowed the Sunday evening walk. At first Mother and Bill, her brother, even accompanied them, but lately Mother and Bill had gone on ahead.

However, Nancy was in a bad humor tonight. "I'll be beneath your level after you're a college fellow," she told him sarcastically.

"Never," he stated flatly. "Let's not waste time arguing. It's almost time for me to go home." John checked his watch under the street light. "All we have done this evening is stand out here and talk about my going to college."

"And our dads," she corrected.

"Let's go inside. I know I'm late for your birthday, but I have a gift for you. I didn't think your mother would like to have me come on a week night to give it to you."

"I don't think she would have minded."

They went indoors, and John took a small package from his pocket. "I'll always think of you at harvest time. Your hair reminds me of wheat ready to harvest."

"Oh!" exclaimed Nancy. "It's beautiful!" She held up the soft white handkerchief with golden wheat sprigs crisscrossed around the boarder.

"That reminded me of your hair too. I got it in Mason City last week when Mother and I went to get some parts for the truck."

After John said good-night and left, Nancy looked at the handkerchief. It was the first gift she had ever gotten from a boy. "John must think quite a bit of me to buy me a gift," she reflected.

She went to her mother's downstairs bedroom and showed her the gift handkerchief before she took it upstairs and placed it with her treasures in a small cedar chest her father had made for her not long before he had died.

"I'll lose John if he goes away to college," Nancy sighed as she prepared for bed.

# CHAPTER 2

In spite of a restless night, Nancy was at her job as early as usual. Even so Mrs. Way had the coffee measured out and the grill hot.

"The harvest crews pulled into town last night," Mrs. Way, her employer, greeted her. "Looks like more men than usual."

Mrs. Way was always happy when the itinerant harvest crews came to town. They meant money in her bulging pocket and diversity from small town topics.

Before long the Way-Side Café was crowded with men with their friendly jokes and laughter.

Having worked in the café two years, Nancy had learned to ignore some remarks that were a little off-color, and also the flirting of some of the men.

Some of the itinerant crew came back each year; others were new. Nancy noticed one new man that looked as though he were in the wrong place. The expensive-looking clothes fit his tall muscular figure as though they were tailor made.

The harvest crews ate breakfast and very late snacks in the café. The farmer having his wheat crop cut furnished the noon and evening meals.

Late in the afternoon old Harvey, the town news carrier, came into the café for his usual cup of coffee and chat.

"The road construction crew's gonna be here in a day or two you know. . . ."

"They going to start the new freeway?" queried Mrs. Way.

"Sure thing," stated Harvey. "They are starting a quarter mile west of Dry Forks and working both ways, north and south. They'll be here a good many months. That'll bring you business."

"I'll need better help than Sue on the evening shift, and when school starts, I'll lose Nancy." Mrs. Way threw up her hands in a helpless gesture. "There are no good waitresses like Nancy around anymore."

Nancy's eight hours were up at three, but when the road crew arrived, Mrs. Way begged Nancy to stay and help make salads.

Twenty-five men from the road crew ate breakfast, lunch, and dinner in the Way-Side Café.

"The harvest crew calls it a late evening snack, but I call it dinner," Mrs. Way complained. "Those men can eat! Nancy, can't you help me out a bit in the evening? Sue is so slow. Tell you what, I'll give you a nickel an hour more for an evening shift of perhaps an hour or two."

10

Mrs. Yoder looked intently at Nancy across the supper table when she told them of Mrs. Way's proposition. "From eight to ten you'd work, but it's dark at ten."

"Oh, I'm not afraid to walk home in the dark," laughed Nancy.

"You know there's always more drinking when the harvest crew's in town," Bill warned. "And with the construction gang—"

"I can take care of myself." Nancy was rather annoyed. After all, Bill was only fifteen, rather young to be offering advice to an eighteen-year-old.

"Bill will have to come to the café and walk home with you." Her mother's words seemed to settle the matter.

Bill arranged with Mr. Harris, his employer, to sweep and stock the shelves at the grocery store in the evening instead of morning. This way he finished about the same time as Nancy.

So it was neatly settled. The arrangement annoyed Nancy. This left Mother home alone in the evening. Mrs. Yoder worked in the laundry every morning. It seemed to Nancy as though Bill and Mother always managed her affairs. Anyway, she would be earning more money, and that's what mattered most to her now.

One evening Nancy finished earlier than usual. When she left the café, Bill was not there.

"Your boyfriend desert you tonight?" The deep voice startled her.

"Oh!" she exclaimed.

"I didn't mean to scare you," said the stranger.

"I'm not scared. I just didn't see you in the shadows." Nancy laughed when she saw to whom the voice belonged.

"I wasn't in the shadows; I followed you out of the café. I'll walk home with you, Nancy," said the handsome harvest hand.

"I am not afraid alone. I don't live far away." Somehow she felt uneasy. "How did you know my name?"

"I'm very observant. After all, I have practically eaten out of your hand for the past three weeks." He was very handsome when he smiled. "Mrs. Way recommends you very highly."

Nancy was secretly glad she had someone with her when they passed Iky's Bar. However, she didn't even know his name. "I'm afraid I'm not as observant as you. I don't know your name."

"Well," he drawled, "my name is Tagolushia Steven Stankiewiez. My friends call me Tag."

"Oh, Mr. Stank-Stank—" Nancy was really embarrassed that she could not even pronounce his name a second after he had said it.

"You better call me Tag like all my friends do," he laughed.

"I'd rather call you Steve."

"OK, but you still didn't answer my question about the boyfriend," the man looked down at her.

"It's my brother who walks home with me every night if that's what you mean."

"Oh," he sighed with relief, "I was afraid a

pretty girl like you would have a boyfriend."

"Here is where I live. Good-night." Nancy hurried into the house. She didn't want her mother to know the man had walked home with her.

After that, Steve always tried to get at one of Nancy's tables. The men tipped well; therefore, Mrs. Way assigned one-half of the tables on the east side to Nancy. Sue took care of the west side. Mrs. Way was forced to employ a new girl to wait on the counter. Business was booming.

"I wish I weren't losing you," Mrs. Way sighed heavily as she approached Nancy late one night. She had kept Nancy later and later each evening. "I could raise your pay ten cents an hour if you'd stay."

Nancy's eyes widened. That was a lot of money to her. "But the harvest crew will be gone next week."

"Not all of them," her employer looked at her oddly. "The road crew will be here at least a year."

Nancy was rather confused, but she said no more. Steve insisted on walking home with her each evening. Bill always waited for her and accompanied them.

"Why don't you go on home, Bill?" Nancy turned on her brother as they entered the house one night after work.

"I can't have you walking home with a stranger," Bill spoke authoritatively.

"Steve isn't a stranger, and besides, who made

you my guardian angel?" retorted Nancy.

"Nancy!" Her mother sounded shocked.

"Is he a Christian?" asked Bill.

"He's a fine gentleman. I wouldn't insult him by asking, and you're always tagging along. How can I ask anything?"

"You needn't be afraid to ask that in front of me."

"Children, let's go to bed. These late hours are making all of us grouchy." Mrs. Yoder did look worn-out.

"You and Bill could go to bed early if you wouldn't insist on treating me like a baby," retorted Nancy. "You can quit work too, Mother, because Mrs. Way is giving me a raise to stay over winter."

"You don't mean you're going to?" Mrs. Yoder and Bill asked in unison.

"Yes, I mean that. I have a good job. There is no reason why I should quit and go to school."

"You have only one year to go," said her mother.

"One year is too long. I won't go back. I'd lose my job for good." Nancy's voice was firm.

"There are other jobs," argued her brother.

"In Dry Forks? I wonder where?"

"The Lord would provide," said Bill.

"Anyway, it's time Mother quit working so hard."

"Nancy, I'm still able to work. I wish you'd reconsider about school and be careful of this man."

"Mother, I'm not marrying Steve just because he's gentleman enough to walk home with me."

"It may lead to more than you think." Her mother paused and then added, "I wish you wouldn't be so friendly with this man."

"I can't run to Mamma every time I meet somebody and ask if I may be friendly with him."

"I didn't mean you should. Just remember, Nancy, you reap what you sow."

"Don't you want me to be happy?"

"That's why I'm so concerned."

"Concerned when I meet a nice gentleman?"

"Is he a Christian, Nancy?"

"You're as bad as Bill. I can't ask—"

"You shouldn't have to ask. It should show."

"Steve's a wonderful person, and everyone is jealous of me. He'll be gone next week anyway; so don't worry." Nancy ran upstairs.

Mrs. Yoder turned sadly and went into her bedroom where she took her troubles to God.

# CHAPTER 3

John Burns approached Nancy one Sunday evening rather reluctantly.

"May I walk home with you?"

"You know you may." Nancy wondered why he asked when it had been an accepted thing for more than a year.

"I thought maybe. . . ." John seemed

confused.

"What's wrong, John?"

"Well, I've been hearing things," John managed to say in embarrassment.

"Like what?"

"You have another boyfriend."

Nancy laughed harshly. "I can't even walk beside someone until tales are afloat about me. Are you going to walk alone all the time when you're at college?" She looked at John.

"It doesn't matter, Nancy, if you still want me to walk home with you."

"Maybe I'd better get used to walking alone," Nancy retorted as she started down the dusty road. Her mother and brother had already gone home as they usually did.

"I won't let you walk alone," said John as he fell into step with her.

"Next week it won't matter to you."

Little was said on that homeward walk. When they had almost reached Nancy's home, a car came speeding from town. Sue, Nancy's co-worker, was apparently out riding with some friends.

\*　　\*　　\*

Nancy was in poor humor at work on Monday. Mrs. Way had changed her work to all evening hours. She started at twelve noon and worked until ten.

Sue approached her while she was tying her

apron. "Aren't you the lucky girl!"

"I don't know what you mean," Nancy was really puzzled.

"I'm on to your tricks. You get your hours changed to evening so Steve can walk home with you. And it isn't enough for you to have Steve hanging onto you. You have another boyfriend on the hook for Sunday nights. I saw you walking last night, and it wasn't with Steve. Wait till I tell him you're two-timing him."

"First of all, Sue, it wasn't my idea to change my hours. My brother makes it his business to accompany me after work every night. The harvest crew left Saturday, so you can breathe easy. Next week John Burns will be a hundred miles from here in college and I'll have no boyfriend." Nancy hurried to wait on a group of ladies that had just seated themselves.

"Don't play innocent." Sue's voice followed Nancy as she went through the door.

Nancy didn't realize what Sue meant until late that evening when Steve entered the café.

"I thought you had gone on," Nancy said to Steve as she approached his table to take the order.

"I was sick and didn't go with the crew." Steve did look ill.

Nancy wondered why he didn't walk home with her, but then, he didn't look up to it.

The next day Sue again spoke to Nancy. "Have a nice date last night?" she snickered.

"I didn't have a date last night."

"Come, now, don't give me that. I know about Steve getting left behind."

"What do you mean, Sue?" Nancy held her by the arm and looked at her sharply.

"Quit pinching me. You know what I mean."

"Steve was ill and. . . ."

"Yeah. Anyone gets sick if he makes a hog of himself at Iky's." Sue said with a harsh laugh.

"Sue! You're just jealous. Don't repeat that gossip. I don't believe Steve ever went into Iky's at all."

"Don't be so naive, Nancy."

That night after Nancy and Bill said good-bye to Steve, Bill said to Nancy, "You just have to quit letting Steve follow us home, Nancy. If you don't get rid of him, I'll tell him he isn't wanted. I won't have a drunkard hanging around."

"You don't believe that, Bill. Sue just started a rumor because she's jealous of me."

"Sis, listen to me, Steve got kicked out of the harvest crew because he was so drunk Saturday they had to carry him out of Iky's."

"Steve doesn't drink, Bill. You should know better than to repeat gossip. You can't order me around. Mind your own business."

"When my own sister chums around with a drunk. . . ."

"That's not true!"

"He isn't a Christian."

"Yes, he is."

"Did he say so?"

"Actions speak louder than words!" Nancy was

really angry.

"Why doesn't he go to church?"

"Just because he doesn't come to our church you say he isn't a Christian," shouted Nancy.

"There is no evidence that he goes anywhere."

Neither had noticed their mother before she spoke, "Let's pray for Steve before we go to bed."

"Everyone is against Steve. He can tell he isn't liked," cried Nancy as she fled upstairs.

Bill and his mother knelt in the living room and prayed.

\*   \*   \*

Steve hung around town for a week doing nothing but walk home with Nancy.

The next Monday it was voiced about that Steve was working with the road crew.

Wednesday Steve came into the café early in the evening.

"See my baby out there," he called to Mrs. Way and Nancy.

He pointed to a yellow Model A roadster standing in front of the café. "How about a ride, Nancy?"

Before Nancy could open her mouth, Mrs. Way spoke. "Go ahead, Nancy, things are slow here this evening."

Nancy felt all the eyes of the town on her as they rode with the wind rushing in their faces.

"Where to, My Fair Lady?" asked Steve.

"Anywhere. Just for a ride. It would be fun to ride in the rumble seat," laughed Nancy.

They had driven around quite some time when Nancy realized they were going west a long way from town.

"Where are we going, Steve?"

"There's a swell place to eat and dance in Sylvan Springs."

"I don't dance and I should be home by ten," said Nancy meekly.

After several miles of silence Steve turned the car around and headed back toward town. "All right. Let's get you home by ten."

It was ten minutes after ten when she bid Steve good-night in front of the house. Mrs. Yoder met her at the door.

"Where have you been?" she asked.

Nancy looked at her in surprise. Then anger filled her voice. "Mother, I am eighteen years of age. I will not have you standing over me as if I were a three-year-old demanding that I account for every move."

"Where's Bill, then?"

"Bill? How would I know? It's not my desire that he meets me every night. It's enough to take care of myself without having to look out for him."

Just then Bill came up the front walk.

"She left work early to go riding with that Steve. I waited and waited. Finally I went inside. As soon as I got inside the door, Mrs. Way shouted to me that she had gone riding with

Steve."

"My affairs are my business," cried Nancy. "If you would just quit coming down to the café every night, everything would be fine."

* * *

Bill stood outside Way-Side Cafe wondering if Nancy had already gone with Steve in his car or if he should wait. Schoolwork was taking more time, and he needed to study tonight. He couldn't wait much longer. Since Steve had gotten the car, he walked home alone most of the time anyway. It didn't seem much use to wait only to be ignored and watch them ride away.

The yellow model A snorted around the corner and stopped.

"Hi, kid!" Steve addressed Bill.

"Good evening." (It was difficult to be courteous to this man.) "How's the job?"

"Fine, fine."

"They stood silent for a while. Abruptly Bill asked, "Are you a Christian? Nancy says you are. I wondered if you'd like to come to our Christian Endeavor program on Sunday night."

Steve was dumbfounded but at last found his voice. "I guess I could if Nancy shows me the way to your church."

"Come to our house for supper, and we'll show you the way to our chapel."

Nancy came out the door. "Looks like you two are having a serious talk."

"Yes, a religious one," was Steve's comment. "Come on, Bill. We may as well continue our talk."

Seldom had Bill had the opportunity to ride in a car such as this. He did ride in it again on the following Sunday night when Steve kept his promise to go to church with the Yoders.

# CHAPTER 4

Nancy glanced at the clock as she scrubbed the grill. Eleven o'clock. Steve had slipped into the café half an hour ago. Now he edged up to the counter.

"Do you have to close up the place every night?" His voice was saturated with impatience.

"I'm through now." Nancy took her sweater from the hook. Evenings were getting cooler.

"It's too nice an evening to be wasted," grumbled Steve. The roadster purred to life and they were off for their nightly spin.

Steve drove on the Dry Forks River road. The river, so often dry, gleamed like a silver ribbon in the moonlight. Steve pulled to the side of the road and stopped the engine. "Pretty, isn't it?"

"Yes," whispered Nancy uneasily. She could hear her mother's voice warning her about the danger of parking in the dark. *It's a temptation the staunchest Christian should not yield to,* Mother and others had told her. But with Steve no harm could come to her.

Suddenly Steve drew Nancy to himself and kissed her.

"Steve, don't do that!" exclaimed the frightened girl.

"Why not?" he laughed.

"I—I—well, just don't," she stammered.

"Don't you love me?"

Nancy's voice refused to function. Tears began to fall. She knew it would make problems either way she answered. "I don't know."

\* \* \*

The breakfast dishes clinked in the dishpan. Soapsuds reached to Nancy's elbow. Mrs. Yoder set the iron down with a light thud.

"Nancy," her mother hesitated before going on, "if Mrs. Way is going to keep you later and later each night, you will have to quit."

"I have to keep my job," she bristled.

"You are supposed to be finished at ten. Four times this week it was two in the morning before you came home."

"Steve brings me home. I'm not alone."

"I know that, Nancy, but that's too late."

"Other couples start their date early in the evening. I don't get to start my date until ten, if I am lucky enough to get off work that early."

"But every night."

"Would you rather I walk home alone?"

"You wouldn't have to. Bill willingly walked home with you until the model A came on the

23

scene."

"What's wrong with having Steve bring me home?"

"I don't like a stranger bringing you home."

"One can hardly call a person a stranger after knowing him five months."

"But what do you know about him besides his name which we can't even pronounce? You don't know his family or anything about him."

"Just because Steve wasn't born in Dry Forks seems to make him evil in the eyes of most people."

"No one has said that, Nancy. However, he is known to drink."

"That's all a lie Sue made up because she's jealous of me. I thought you would be the last person to listen to gossip," stormed Nancy. "If you'd only learn to know him."

"Bring him home so that I can get acquainted with him."

\* \* \*

Evenings slipped by so swiftly. Steve was a lot of fun. Nancy wished, however, that they wouldn't park on Dry Forks River road so often. There didn't seem to be much else to do. Steve wouldn't go to church and the parties that her friends gave. She continually refused to go to movies and dances with him. Now she was beginning to wonder if it wouldn't be better to go to a movie occasionally. How long could she

24

prevent more trouble?

"Mother is getting quite upset because we see so much of each other," Nancy told Steve one night. "Please come into the house when you bring me home or call for me."

"Would that suit her? Bill thinks I'm poison."

"They just don't know you, Steve. If you would go to church with me on Sunday evenings, they wouldn't think you were so bad."

"I'll compromise. If you go to the places I like, I'll go to church every Sunday evening."

Nancy remained silent a long time. She tried to pray, but God seemed far away. She just couldn't give Steve up now after all the months of companionship. "All right," she whispered.

Steve kept his promise, and soon it was an accepted thing for Nancy to go to the Saturday night movie after she was finished working.

Steve seemed almost to enjoy going to church on Sunday evening. He was learning to know many of the people at church.

"Is that a husband and wife?" he asked as Stella Martin drove the ancient car to the door of the church and helped her father into it.

"Oh, no," laughed Nancy. "It's a father and his daughter." Then her face sobered. "Poor Gaylord Martin is only about fifty, but he has grieved for his wife so many years that he looks like an old man."

"It is sad when a young woman dies."

"She didn't die." Nancy hesitated before adding, "She ran away with another man."

"He should remarry instead of grieving for a no-good wife."

"Mr. Martin is a fine Christian."

"What does that have to do with it?"

"'What . . . God hath joined together, let not man put asunder,'" quoted Nancy. She glanced sideways at Steve. "We don't believe in divorce at our church."

"That's silly. You mean he'd go through life alone just because—well—because of a silly church rule?" Steve almost stopped the car to look at her.

"The Bible says that."

"I thought the program was very nice tonight," said Steve.

"Yes, I enjoyed it," stammered Nancy.


# CHAPTER 5

"Must we go to church tonight?" Steve's voice was like a whining child's.

"That was the agreement. I thought you said you enjoyed the services last Sunday evening."

"I did. But every Sunday is too much."

"Why?"

"Don't always ask why, Nancy."

"What better could we do than go to church?"

"Let's go to Sylvan Springs."

"What for?" Nancy's voice was sharp.

"Don't snap at me like that, or I'll leave and

you can go to church alone. Aren't there churches in Sylvan Springs?"

"It's too late to go that far. I'm sorry I snapped at you. We can go there next Sunday evening."

Reluctantly Steve turned the car toward the Dry Forks Chapel.

"That preacher doesn't like me. He's always asking silly questions after the service. I'd rather go to a larger church," grumbled Steve.

"Let's hurry. The house is full and we're late."

"My text this evening is found in 2 Corinthians 6:14." Elmer Burns paused to wait for Nancy and Steve to slip into seats in the back of the church. "Be ye not unequally yoked together with un-believers: for what fellowship hath righteousness with unrighteousness? and what communion hath light with darkness?"

The sermon was well prepared. Nancy shifted to the left. Steve sat rigid. Nancy shifted uncomfortably to the right. *How will Steve react to a sermon like this? Someone must have told the minister about my dating a non-Christian*, she thought as she squirmed around again.

"Sit still," commanded Steve into her ear. "You have the preacher looking at us all the time."

At last the sermon was over, and they slipped out quickly without meeting anyone.

At home after Steve left, Nancy confronted her mother. "You told Elmer Burns to preach a sermon *at* me. You just want to drive Steve away."

"I didn't speak to anyone about your affairs. This was probably God's way of speaking to you, and your conscience is bothering you."

Mrs. Yoder could not convince Nancy that she had not told the preacher she was dating a non-Christian.

Nancy did not even ask Steve to go to church with her the next Sunday evening.

Mrs. Way solved this problem. She demanded that Nancy help at the café every Sunday evening. The idea was a bit repelling at first, but then she saw this as an outlet to avoid going to church on Sunday evening. It seemed as though the minister always preached at her.

Lately Nancy had been too tired to go to church on Sunday morning. There seemed to be plenty of time, however, to park on the river road. She refused to yield to Steve's advances.

One cold November night Steve was irritable because Nancy had had to work overtime again. The roadster furnished little warmth. "Come on over close to me," Steve ordered.

When Nancy did not move, he moved close to her. Roughly he took her in his arms.

"Steve! Stop it!" she ordered. She pushed Steve away.

Suddenly Steve was very angry. "You lead a fellow on, and then you slap him down," he said fiercely. "You don't love me at all."

"Steve, I do love you. Let's quit sneaking around like this. Why can't we be married and have a home?"

"I don't have enough money to get married."

"I have a little saved. I'm willing to go on working, and I'm willing to live in a few rooms until we can afford something better. Love is working together too."

This was not the only evening they talked of marriage.

One night Steve startled Nancy.

"Do you love me enough to keep our marriage a secret for a little while?"

"Why, Steve?"

"Must you always ask why?" he sounded cross. "First of all, your mom doesn't like me nor your smart-alecky brother. Then I have some private reasons."

"I should meet your family first. I'd like to have a nice wedding in the church and have our families—"

"No!" shouted Steve. "If you love me, you'll take me on my terms."

"All right. All right. Don't get so excited."

"Let's plan on Saturday then. You ask Mrs. Way to let you off. No, let me ask her. She likes me. I'll tell her we're going to Sylvan Springs. She'll be glad to see you having a good time for a change. Don't you tell a soul."

Glad that she was to be spared the added sin of lying to her employer, Nancy readily agreed to let Steve make the arrangements.

\* \* \*

Nancy was nervous by the time they arrived at Mason City. "Let's look for a minister."

"No," said Steve shortly. "You wanted to get married, so you'll have to be satisfied with short-notice arrangements.

"We do need to buy a license in this state," he stated rather grudgingly.

They quickly discovered that Saturday noon just before quitting time was not a good time to buy a license. The man at the desk was in poor humor.

"Come on, speak up," he growled at Nancy. "Age?"

"Eighteen." She tried to still her hands from shaking.

"You're older than eighteen, I hope. A man has to be twenty-one in this state," he said, turning to Steve.

"I'm forty years old, sir."

Nancy thought she would faint. She knew Steve was older but never imagined that he was forty. *He doesn't even have gray hair*, she thought, looking at the blond wavy hair she had always admired.

In the car at last Nancy spoke. "Are you really forty years old?"

"Why would I lie about my age? What's the matter with forty?" he demanded.

"It just never occurred to me how old you are. It seems strange that you are so handsome and—and—well, that you never married before."

"There's lots of strange things in this world. Let's get this over and done with." Steve brought the car to a halt in front of the "Justice of the Peace" sign.

# CHAPTER 6

Married life was far different from what Nancy had expected. She longed to share her happy secret with someone but dared not. Every time she spoke about it to Steve he got so angry.

She had a hard time convincing herself she was married when she and Steve drove out on the Dry Forks River road just as they always had. Steve kept reminding her she had wanted legal papers.

It was snowing the night Steve failed to pick her up after work. She hurried home in the cold raw air. Sleep would not come. What terrible accident had prevented him from coming for her tonight?

Sue hinted the next day at work. "Steve sure was sick again last night, wasn't he?"

"It's none of your business if Steve picks me up or not. We had previous arrangements."

"You mean he was soaked that early in the evening he couldn't keep his date with you!" she exclaimed.

"Keep your filthy tongue still." Nancy spoke through clenched teeth. "You're just jealous."

"There's nothing to be jealous of. I got a boyfriend that drinks as much as Steve."

"I said 'be quiet!'"

Nancy refused to speak to Sue for many weeks.

Steve did not come to take her home for three nights in succession. It had not occurred to Nancy before that she actually did not know where Steve stayed.

When Steve finally did come to take her home again, she scolded him. "I should be taking care of you when you're sick, and I don't even know where you are staying."

"Don't try to find out either," he told her angrily.

"But, Steve, I'm your wife now. . . ."

"Don't ever say that out loud again," shouted Steve. "You stick by your agreement. Do you hear?"

"All right, but don't shout at me. I can hear. I guess you'll have to take care of yourself when you're sick."

\* \* \*

When the harvest crew caame to town in June Steve joined them again. It was not the same crew he'd been with the year before. The days were busy, and Nancy dropped into bed bone weary every night.

There was little time for Mother and Bill to nag at her about allowing Steve to escort her home every night.

\* \* \*

It was a hot afternoon and business was slow when John Burns came into the café.

He ordered iced tea for two and asked Nancy to join him. She was uneasy lest Steve find her there. She had never told him about John.

"They tell me you have a new boyfriend." John lost no time in getting to the point.

"What's that to you?" bristled Nancy.

"Nothing. Only he's not a Christian, is he? And you're not coming to church anymore."

"You're all alike. Just because you are jealous, you pick on him." Nancy stood up spilling her tea.

"Nancy, don't be foolish."

"I'm foolish because I want to be happy. I wish you'd leave me alone. You were too selfish to care. You had to run away to college when you could have stayed home and worked toward a home of your own. You didn't care then if I'd be lonesome. It's too late now. Go and leave me alone." She fled to the kitchen for a cloth and began wiping the spilled tea.

"Just let me say I've prayed for you and I'll keep on praying." John left without drinking his tea.

Nancy was hardly in the car that evening when Steve spoke. "So you entertained a boyfriend this afternoon."

"Who told you that?"

"Does it matter who? The story'd be the same wouldn't it?" Steve sneered. "You served him iced tea on the house."

Nancy hadn't thought of it before that John had forgotten to pay for the tea he had ordered.

"Sue must have been around. She always has been jealous of me and wanted to cause you to be cross at me. I hope she told you we had a fight and neither of us drank the tea that he forgot to pay for." Nancy sighed. She was so tired.

"You're my wife now, so let other men alone."

"Don't say that out loud, Steve. You know the agreement." Steve laughed then.

The days seemed so long for Nancy. She could hardly get out of bed in the morning. She was glad when the time came to quit work. A few nights she begged Steve to take her home right after work.

This night dark thunderclouds were forming in the northeast as they drove on the Dry Forks river road.

"Nancy, could you loan me a little money? A harvest hand doesn't get paid until the end of the run, you know."

"No, I didn't know that. What do you need money for, and how much do you need?"

"Do I have to give an account of every penny? After all, you're my wife. I need clothes badly."

"How much? I have to draw it out of my savings account."

"How much do you have in your savings account?" asked Steve.

"Around two thousand dollars. But you certainly don't need that much for clothes." She looked at him in alarm.

"No," laughed Steve, "two or three hundred will see me through."

"Two or three hundred! For clothes!"

"Be stingy then. When I get my pay I won't share it with you either."

Nancy drew two hundred and fifty dollars from her savings account the next morning. She gave it to Steve Saturday night.

"Thanks, sweetheart. This is only a loan. I'll pay it back in November or December."

"November or December!"

"That's when a harvest hand gets paid, you know—when harvest is over."

"Where is harvest over in December?"

"North. Surely you know that all crews work northward into Canada."

"No, I didn't know. How will you get your money? Is the crew boss honest enough to see that you get your money?" she asked in alarm.

"Surely, my dear," Steve began evenly, "you realize when a harvest hand signs up, it is for the season."

"The season!"

"Yes. I go for the duration as long as there is wheat to harvest."

"No, Steve, you can't."

"Of course I can," he laughed.

* * *

As the harvest crews began to leave town one by one, Nancy hoped Steve would be sick again and be left behind.

After a week had gone by and he did not meet

her, Nancy knew that Steve had not been left behind. He hadn't even bid her good-bye.

She cried herself to sleep every night. "Where, oh, where is Steve?" her heart cried. "Why was I so foolish as to consent to a secret marriage?"

# CHAPTER 7

Nancy hurried home alone each night until one night her brother met her at the corner of Main and Easly Street.

"Alone and walking tonight, Sis?" Bill's voice registered surprise.

"Steve's been gone a week already."

"Well, I hope he is gone for good."

"Bill! He isn't. I'm sure."

"How come you're so sure?"

"I just am. He'll be back as soon as harvest is over."

"Those harvest crews keep following the harvest north as late as October."

"I know. Steve told me he may not be back before late in the fall, but when you sign up with a crew, you have to finish with them."

"You do? I didn't know that. How come he didn't have to last year?"

"You know very well he was sick." She always got angry when Bill spoke about Steve.

"Yes. I guess he was sick at that."

"You still believe the old gossip about Steve drinking. I wish you'd try to learn to know him better. Then you'd know he doesn't drink more than ordinary."

"More than ordinary," Bill screeched. "What's ordinary drinking?"

"Well, everyone tastes liquor once in a lifetime," was Nancy's weak reply.

"I never intend to taste a drop," stated Bill emphatically. "Just how well do you think you know Steve?"

"Well enough," was her vague answer.

"Does he have a family? Where are they? Where does he come from?"

"Hold on. What does his family have to do with it? I'm not marrying the family."

"Marrying!" Bill's voice almost failed him. "You're not thinking of marrying the man?"

"I mean if I did," stammered Nancy.

"You can't mean you'd marry a fellow without knowing more about him?" asked Bill incredulously.

"Forget it." Nancy ran ahead slamming the front door.

*   *   *

Nancy was really in a predicament. At times it seemed as though she had to tell her mother what she had done, and the next minute she thought she would rather die than tell anyone.

Nancy seemed to be ill and had to take off from

37

work so many days. One Friday morning she felt better after a few hours' sleep. Nancy started downstairs to find something to eat. She was surprised to find her mother ironing.

"How come you're home, Mother?"

"I've been home every day for two months since I quit at the laundry. I iron for several families. This way I can sit down or even lie down to rest when I'm tired. You haven't taken enough interest in your home lately."

Nancy sat staring into space a long time. Finally her mother spoke again.

"Where is Steve?"

"Why?"

"Steve has gotten you into trouble and run off?"

"Steve didn't run off, Mother."

"Bill says he left."

"He's coming back. I knew he was leaving. He had to keep his contract."

"Where is he? Does he write to you?"

"He'll be back."

"When is he coming back?" demanded Mrs. Yoder.

After a long silence, "You may as well face it, Nancy. Steve won't come back and marry you. . . ."

"He doesn't have to come back to marry me."

"It will be a blessing if he doesn't."

"Mother, how can you say such a thing!" exclaimed Nancy. "I love Steve and—and—"

"He certainly can't love you to leave you in

this condition."

"You may as well know now as anytime. There is no shame about it. Steve and I are married," cried Nancy. Tears had been close to the surface and now spilled over.

"Married! Married!" Nancy's mother sat down on the closest chair. "Nancy, you can't mean it!" Her face was white, and she was trembling. "Nancy, you can't mean that."

"Yes, I mean it, Mother. You should feel better that I'm not bringing shame on the Yoder name." Even Nancy's voice sounded weary.

"The name matters little. It's you that counts. I just can't believe that you secretly married him." Her mother was still stunned. "Why, Nancy, did you do it?"

"I love Steve. What's so unusual about that?"

"But why did it have to be a secret?"

"You would never have consented. Bill fusses every time he sees me with Steve."

"A marriage that has to be kept secret has something wrong with it from the start."

"I believe you are wishing me grief. Why is everyone against Steve? Just because he didn't happen to be born in Dry Forks?" Nancy's tears began anew. "Besides Steve had personal reasons for keeping our marriage a secret," she finished lamely.

"Whatever are we going to do?"

"Do? I don't know what you mean?"

"I guess I don't either." Mrs. Yoder put her head down on her arms on the table and cried.

Nancy began to realize how foolish she had been, and she was sorry for what she had done.

At last Mrs. Yoder raised her head and spoke. "I promised your father I'd take care of you children. I never felt I could do it alone. But we are not alone. God will help me, and I hope you will choose to let Him help you too."

\* \* \*

It was easier for Nancy after her secret was known. She could sleep better, and work seemed easier when she felt more rested.

One night at quitting time, Mrs. Way approached her. "How long are you planning to work yet, Nancy?" she asked bluntly.

"I—I don't know what you mean," Nancy managed to stammer.

"In a public place like the café we can't have you around much longer," she snapped. "You aren't fooling anyone. You're hurting trade. Decent people won't eat here if I keep a single girl in your condition around."

"I am not a single girl, Mrs. Way. Steve and I were married six months ago."

"Oh, sure!" she exclaimed nastily. "How come he left you alone?"

"Steve's coming back when he's through harvesting."

"Yes. Where's he now?"

"In Montana," she lied. If only she did know where Steve was, it wouldn't be so hard.

Nancy's homeward-bound feet were heavy.

She realized that she held in her hand the last paycheck she would receive for some time. She didn't want to ask her mother to keep her without paying her way. What would she do? Five months of no work could use up savings fast. She had to buy her little one clothes. Tears were falling fast when her brother met her.

Bill had no solution to offer. "You reap what you sow, Sis." But he put his arm across her shoulder in a brotherly manner, something he hadn't done for a long time.

# CHAPTER 8

Nancy determined that she would not use her savings unless she were flat on her back, nor would she be a burden to her mother. She had boasted to John Burns that she didn't want to leave her mother when she could make life easier for her.

The job Nancy finally found was ideal for her. Doctor Randall, the dentist, wanted someone to clean his offices three evenings a week after office hours.

Nancy helped her mother with the ironing enough so that she felt she was earning her board. She was overjoyed when Mrs. McAllister, the neighbor who had taken her place at the café, asked her to do her laundry and ironing as well as clean her house once a week.

*    *    *

The daylight hours grew shorter. September faded into October. Since it was Bill's senior year, he spent many of the long evening hours in his room studying when he wasn't working at Harris's grocery store.

The night was cold for October. Nancy took her coat from the living room closet. It was too snug, so she hung it up again.

"Were you going somewhere?" inquired her mother.

"The stores are open tonight. I thought I'd do a little shopping."

"Would you like me to go with you?"

"It would make you too tired to walk that far."

"Five blocks! Well, I guess not. If you want me I'll go along."

As soon as they returned from their shopping trip, Nancy spread the soft white material and tiny pattern pieces on the table. She emptied one of her own drawers, and each evening a tiny new garment found its place with the rest.

*Why doesn't Steve come back?* Nancy wondered as she sat on her mother's low rocker looking at the snowflakes fly. *The last day of November already. Is Mother right? Will Steve ever come back? How could he have meant to desert me when he didn't even know about the baby?*

Sundays seemed endless. She didn't want to go to church, and what if Steve came while she wasn't at home?

*Perhaps Steve will come tomorrow,* thought Nancy.

"Bill," she started to speak hesitatingly one Saturday, "if I give you the money, will you get a duck besides the usual groceries?"

"Sure," said Bill jovially. "Is the preacher coming to Sunday dinner or something?"

Nancy turned her back but it was too late to hide the tears. She didn't want to tell her brother she hoped Steve would come.

"That's all right, Sis," said Bill soberly. "We can have roast duck anytime."

The time passed more quickly on Sunday morning when she stuffed and roasted the duck. The nice stew with carrots, onions, and potatoes took more time than the soup and cold meat they'd been accustomed to eating for Sunday dinner. But there was Sunday afternoon and the long evening to be lived through.

The rocker creaked in the twilight as Nancy was once again in her usual position. *How will I ever live until April if Steve doesn't come,* she wondered to herself.

*There he is—walking and all covered with snow.* Eagerly she ran to the front door, opened it, and peered at the tall figure ladened with packages coming up the front walk.

"Say, that's a swell welcome," laughed Bill. "My hands were too full to open the front door."

A sob caught in Nancy's throat. "I wasn't sure who it was."

"I guess I do look funny. Can you sweep some of the snow off before I come in?"

If Bill saw her tears he didn't mention it. "Hey, Mom," he called as he entered the living room, "where's our Christmas tablecloth? Here it is the day before Christmas and no preparations made."

Nancy sat on the rocker again. "I'd forgotten about Christmas."

"We can't do that," boomed Bill.

Mrs. Yoder hurried to the buffet and took out her best red-checked cloth. She busied herself spreading the cloth before she put two packages on the table. Bill placed his nicely-wrapped packages on the table. "Now let's eat supper. I'm hungry."

Christmas morning was clear and cold. The aroma of chicken roasting wakened Nancy. *I must have been tired. It's nearly nine o'clock.* Slowly she dressed and dragged herself downstairs.

"No church on Christmas morning?" she inquired as she stepped fron the stair landing.

Her mother and Bill sat reading.

"We decided not to go," said Bill.

"Let me get you some breakfast." Mrs. Yoder bustled about the kitchen.

When breakfast was over, Bill told them to come into the living room. "Do you still know Luke 2:8-20, Nancy?"

She nodded. They all repeated the passage together.

Tearfully Nancy stroked the soft woolly slippers that her mother had knit for her and then put them on her feet.

Slowly she unwrapped the packages Bill had placed on her lap. The gray sweater Bill had chosen for his mother just suited her.

Nancy held up her sweater from her brother. "Green—just the right shade to go with my hair."

The other package contained the softest, whitest yarn Nancy had ever seen. "How could you ever find such nice yarn for me?" she cried.

Bill cleared his throat in embarrassment. He picked up the knitting needles and book, *Pretty Things for Baby*, that had slipped to the floor.

"Don't all mothers knit soft fancy things?" he asked.

"Yes." Nancy's face brightened. Although she had learned to knit when she was quite young, she had not done so for a number of years. She would not disappoint Bill. She would start right now.

"I had help in choosing the yarn," offered Bill, his face coloring. "Sally Hale works at the dime store in the evening and Saturdays. She helped me choose the things."

"You think a lot of Sally, don't you?"

"She's a fine Christian girl," said Bill, "and she has good taste, doesn't she?"

"Yes, any girl who looks your way more than once has good taste."

"Aw, I meant the yarn and things." They both laughed. Mrs. Yoder smiled. It was good to see them laugh.

Only the tiny white sweater and one bootie were finished when Nancy's baby girl was born. It was a cold but sunny day in January. "How wonderful to start a new year with a new baby," thought Nancy.

The hospital was in Sylvan Springs, 23 miles from Dry Forks. Bill and Mother could not come to visit her very often.

Nancy lay in bed resting. She was too ill to think much about Steve for a few days.

One day Dr. Braddock looked at her gravely, "You seem to be gaining a little strength. You may be moved into the ward if you still want the cheaper room."

"Yes, please," Nancy said weakly, "I need to economize."

There were twelve mothers in the ward. Every four hours the nurse brought the babies in to be fed.

"Nurse, why can't I feed my baby like the rest of the mothers?"

"Ask your doctor," replied the nurse and hurried away.

The evenings were terrible when all the other women had a husband chatting happily by their bedsides.

The next day Nancy asked, "Doctor Braddock, when can I see my baby?"

"What's your baby's name?"

"Nola Joy. But—"

"That's a pretty name. Be a good girl and rest a lot." The doctor was gone.

The next day the doctor seemed extra cheerful when he came in. "You may sit up today and tomorrow. In a day or two you'll be walking around."

"Doctor," cried Nancy, "you must tell me what's wrong with my baby."

"She only weighed three pounds, you know," was the brusque reply.

At the end of two weeks Nancy felt she could hardly leave the hospital and leave Nola Joy behind. Her arms ached to hold her baby.

Worst of all was the loneliness and ache in her heart. "If only Steve were here," grieved Nancy, "I could bear it better."

Nancy knew that Nola would never wear the soft knit garments. There was no need to finish the booties.

Because Elmer Burns was a minister, he was one of the few in the Dry Forks area who had a telephone. Nancy was grief-stricken when he brought the message that her baby was gone.

"God is punishing me," sobbed Nancy bitterly.

"If that were true," the minister spoke softly, "how greatly we would all suffer. 'There is none righteous, no, not one.' We'd fare poorly, Nancy, if God would punish us like this for our mistakes."

Elmer Burns took care of all the arrangements. Sally Hale came to stay with Nancy while Bill and his mother attended the short graveside service.

Nancy lay still on her bed.

"Can I do anything for you, Nancy?" asked

Sally.

Nancy was silent for a long time. Then she got up. She took the small bottie from her knitting bag. The sweater had been put on the baby. "Put the knitting bag way back on the top shelf of the closet, please, where I'll not need to see it for a long time."

Obediently Sally climbed on a chair and tucked into a remote corner of the closet the knitting bag containing the remaining yarn that she had helped Bill choose for his sister.

Nancy took the bootie and a small cedar chest and sat on the edge of her bed. "My daddy made this little chest for me just before he died," she explained to Sally, "and these are my treasures: my first Testament, a pin I received from my first-grade teacher for outstanding work, my baptismal certificate, and this handkerchief which is the only gift I ever got from a boy. John Burns gave it to me for my eighteenth birthday because it reminded him of my hair and ripened wheat ready for harvesting."

Nancy put the bootie in the chest with her other treasures.

"I'm reaping only tears," cried Nancy. "Don't ever be as foolish as I have been."

Sally put her arms about Nancy and silently wept with her. At last she spoke. "You can come back to God."

"How can I come back to God when He has taken away my baby and Steve?"

"God didn't take Steve away. He left of his own

accord. The baby could have died even if you had been the best of Christians and never strayed."

"Steve must be dead too or he would come back," sobbed Nancy. "He must have met with an accident or something."

"We'll pray for him, Nancy."

Two days after the funeral Pastor Burns called on Nancy and her mother. The neighbors had all been so kind and offered to help in any way.

"I have a small gift for you, Nancy." He handed her an envelope containing money.

"I won't accept charity," she told him. "I paid all my bills, and I will soon be able to work again. If I'd accept it, you would expect me to come to your church."

"Not at all, Nancy. We do hope you will see your way clear to attend church soon, but that's not the idea. We help anyone in the community regardless of church affiliation. This is from your neighbors. I was asked to bring it because I am a preacher. Seems like preachers are asked to do this type of thing."

Nancy knew this to be true, but she would not accept the money. She went up to her room crying.

After considering silently for a time, Pastor Burns handed the envelope to Mrs. Yoder. "Put it in a fund for her. Someday she will be glad for it. I can't take it back and tell them she doesn't want it."

"Thank them for it." Mrs. Yoder put it in her apron pocket.

# CHAPTER 9

Nancy lay listless on the bed day after day. Finally her mother asked Doctor Braddock to come and see her.

After a close check he spoke to Mrs. Yoder in the kitchen. "She is a bit run down physically. I've left a tonic. I think her main problem is grief. Where is the father of her child?"

Mrs. Yoder faced the doctor. "I don't know, and I'm sure Nancy doesn't know where he is."

"She may be worrying about the bills. He should be made to foot the bills."

"Nancy had some money saved. The bills are all paid."

"She claims he is her husband?"

"Yes. I saw the papers."

"Maybe the best thing for Nancy would be to find a job. Keeping busy is sometimes the best medicine."

Nancy wanted to work in the café, but Mrs. Way had enough help. Mrs. Randall was glad to have someone to clean the dentist's offices again. Mrs. McAllister wanted Nancy to take care of her laundry and house. There were others who wanted to have some housecleaning done also. She worked a different place every day.

She had to do a lot of walking but the color began coming back to her face, and there was new life in her step.

One day Mrs. Randall asked, "Nancy, would

you have time to really scrub the three rooms up here?" She beckoned for her to follow her up the stairs into the reception hall. "We'd like to get them ready to rent."

So each week Nancy scrubbed a room in the tiny apartment above the dentist's offices.

The kitchen was a mere hall with cupboards lining the one wall except for a tiny window over the sink that faced a side street. The cupboards were a dull gray and badly scuffed.

*Yellow paint would brighten it up,* she thought as she scrubbed. *Along the other side one could put a small table.*

The living room was large, and three windows in a row faced Main Street. Nancy liked to sew. She thought she could make a nice slipcover for the faded sofa that stood in one corner. A plan began forming in her mind. *I'll ask Mrs. Randall next week.*

"That would be nice, Nancy. I did not know your husband was coming home. Yes, if you paint and fix it up as you told me, you may have it for ten dollars a month and the first two months rent-free."

Nancy's mother was shocked. "Why do you feel you must leave, Nancy?"

"I'm sure Steve will come back, and I want to have a little nest ready. He wouldn't come here anyway."

The color and sparkle in Nancy's face pleased her mother, so she thought perhaps it might be good for her, but she wondered what would happen if Steve didn't return. Mrs. Yoder shuddered.

June brought graduation for Bill, and immediately he left for Mason City to take a six-week course in business administration.

"Will you stay with Mother while I'm gone?" asked Bill.

A week after Bill had gone the harvest crews came to town again. Mrs. Way asked Nancy to come back and help to serve breakfast and lunch. Nancy was eager. She liked waitress work better than cleaning and ironing.

It was hot for June, and there were more men in the harvest crews than usual.

"I'm really tired," sighed Nancy to herself, "but I must go by and check the apartment. There's part of a roast that will spoil over Sunday." Nancy and her mother had stayed in the apartment all week because it was only a block from the café. Tonight they were going to stay at her mother's because it was closer to the church.

"Let's see, the windows are closed." She was talking to herself as she checked when a knock sounded. *Callers? No one knows I'm here but Mrs. Way.*

"Steve," was all she could say when she opened the door. "Steve!"

He stepped inside the door and grabbed her by the shoulders. Shaking her furiously he growled, "Nancy, you agreed to keep our marriage secret. I come back and everyone knows. What's the big idea anyway? Speak up before I slap you good and proper."

Nancy was completely surprised and hurt. She opened her mouth to speak but no words came.

"Well?" Steve towered over her.

"I can't talk when you shout and shake your fist in my face. Can I help it if you didn't keep your part of the bargain?" Nancy's voice shook.

"My part of the bargain! Just what is my part of the bargain?"

"You went away."

"When did I ever agree I'd live under your thumb? Tell me when and what I agreed to."

Nancy shook her head. She could not remember any promises he had made. "It's only normal for a man to live with his wife, Steve. If you love me. . . ."

"It was your idea to get married. I would have been satisfied without bothering to get married."

"Steve!" she retorted angrily. "I wasn't brought up that way."

"According to your brother and the preacher, you weren't brought up to go out with a non-Christian either." Steve laughed unkindly.

"I've paid dear for it too."

"What do you mean?"

"Hasn't anyone told you why I had to tell?"

"Why?"

"No one told you about our baby?"

"And you *had* to tell?"

"Why should it be such a secret?" Nancy slumped wearily on a chair.

Steve threw his head back and laughed. "Still

the same Nancy, full of questions. If you'd have taken my advice, all this fuss wouldn't be necessary."

Nancy wasn't sure what Steve meant. "Steve, don't you even care about your own child?"

"What child?"

"Our baby girl that died. We would have told you if we had known where you were."

"Nancy, remember I was a harvest hand when you met me, and that's the way it is. It's just as well you don't have a little one. They are too expensive. Now get me some supper."

"Oh, Steve." She could hardly believe anyone could speak like that about his own child. She got supper and cleaned up the dishes. It was nine o'clock before she finished. Steve was asleep on the sofa.

"Steve," she called softly, "Bill is away attending business school, and Mother is alone. She and I had been staying together at night. . . ."

"Well you can't go over there tonight. It won't hurt her to be alone."

"At least I'll have to go and tell her where I am. She was expecting me home after work. I only came by here to get some food out of the refrigerator."

"Go tell her then," he growled.

"Would you please take me? It's dark now."

"Take you," he shouted. "Can't you walk? No. Go on and tell your mamma, and then get home to bed."

# CHAPTER 10

Even though Saturday was a busy day at Way-Side Café, Nancy tried to make something special for supper on Saturday evening.

"I hear your man's at home," greeted Mr. Harris as she entered the grocery store.

"Yes. He came with the first harvest crew."

"I have some nice fryers here. Steve likes chicken."

"M-m-m. Fried chicken, gravy, mashed potatoes. Do you have one the right size for two?"

"Here's the bird for you. Sure glad that man of yours came back."

Nancy hurried home. The apartment needed a bit of cleaning. She sang as she worked. "Sure is hot. I wouldn't be surprised we're in for a storm," she told herself as she looked at the clouds in the west.

It was dusk when she decided to wash the stack of cooking utensils. From the window over the sink she saw the crew boss's pickup ramble into town. Steve was on the front seat between Mr. Johnson, the crew boss, and another man. Hurriedly she made the gravy.

The table looked so nice. Grandma Kuntz had given her some white begonia blossoms. The yellow tablecloth matched the sunshine yellow cupboards. On the windowsill stood the chocolate cake. Nancy touched it lightly. *It's cool enough to frost. Steve will be along any minute* now. *Mr. Johnson could have let him off in front of the house instead of making him walk from the rooming house since he was driving right past.*

She looked at the clock as she finished the last swirl of icing. *Chocolate has always been Steve's favorite cake. I wonder what's keeping him.*

Half an hour later Nancy decided she'd have to reheat the chicken. *Maybe I was mistaken, but it looked like Steve in the middle front seat of Mr. Johnson's truck.*

By eight o'clock Nancy was really irritated. She filled the dishpan with hot water, turned the burner on low, and placed the kettle of mashed potatoes in the water over the burner. "If he isn't here in a few minutes," she said aloud, "I'll have to make fried potato cakes. They're stiff and lumpy now."

"I'll go down and see." Rapidly Nancy descended the stairs of the apartment. She looked toward the east. The street was deserted. Stopping on the doorstep she reflected, *Why must the hired hands work so late when the crew boss doesn't?*

Time seemed to drag. At last she walked to the corner. Mrs. Compton's rooming house, where many of the harvest crew stayed, was two blocks north. Just then a man came out, got in the truck, and came toward Main Street.

*Maybe I can ask Mr. Johnson.*

Mr. Johnson drove to the café and went inside. *What shall I do?*

Nancy waited and then walked the two blocks

west toward the Way-Side Café. She could see Mr. Johnson in the far corner eating at a table by himself. She also noticed that the clock over the counter said fifteen minutes until nine.

Nancy went inside and walked to Mr. Johnson's table.

"Excuse me, Mr. Johnson," she started to speak timidly, "could you please tell me why Steve has to work so late?"

Mr. Johnson looked at her, a bite of steak midway to his mouth. "Madam, he got out of my truck three hours ago. Iky's is the only place to find him on payday. I miss my guess if you don't have to carry him out."

Stunned, Nancy stared at the man. "Payday!" she blurted. "I thought harvesters get paid when harvest is over!"

"My crew'd all starve that way, Madam. I work north into Canada then go back to Mexico and start all over. Harvest is seldom done for my crew."

Nancy fled from the café. She sped home and flung herself on the sofa. The food stood in the heat of the tiny kitchen as Nancy cried and cried.

\* \* \*

Pounding awakened Nancy. She sat up trying to think where she was. "Open up, or we'll bust the door down," shouted a rough male voice.

Trembling, Nancy looked at the clock. *Who could it be at three o'clock in the morning?*

57

"Open the door. We've got our hands full."

When Nancy opened the door, two men carried Steve into the room.

"What happened?"

"Anybody who drinks as much as this fellow is bound to be in bad shape. Next time you'll come and get him yourself." They dumped Steve on the sofa and left.

Nancy thought she would be sick. She had never seen anyone in such a deplorable condition. Slowly she labored to get his filthy clothes off him.

She took the clothes into the kitchen. While she heated water to wash the clothes she took the things from the pockets. His wallet and handkerchief, a few coins. She laid ninety cents on the table. From the shirt pocket she took an envelope.

"Steve's pay envelope dated July 7, 1929. That's today. Yesterday," she corrected herself mentally as she noticed again the clock which now said four o'clock.

Impulsively Nancy took up the wallet. It was empty. Not a bill or penny in it. The ninety cents on the table appeared to be all that was left from a pay envelope that indicated on the outside it had once contained forty-five dollars, a week's wages.

A photograph fluttered from the wallet. As Nancy picked it up, soft eyes smiled at her from the picture of a lady holding a baby. A small boy stood beside her. It was worn so badly Nancy could scarcely read the scrawled writing on the back of the photo. *Steven 3, Da— months old.* There was a break and dirt across the name and age of the smaller child. Apparently Steve had a younger brother. *I wonder if his mother and brother are still living, and where is his dad?*

* * *

Wednesday evening after a late supper Nancy sat in the living room mending Steve's shirt while he lay on the sofa nearby.

"Steve, when is your birthday?"

"Always questions. What do you want to know that for?"

"I'd get you a new shirt for your birthday if it were soon."

"Well, you wouldn't have to wait for my birthday. But I buy my own clothes. You give me the money."

"You got paid Saturday. What did you do with all your money?"

"Who told you I got paid on Saturday?" shouted Steve. He was on his feet now. "Who said I got paid?"

"You needn't shout at me. I saw the envelope, and Mr. Johnson said—"

"When did you talk to Mr. Johnson? Don't you ever meddle in my affairs again. Do you hear me?"

"I'm your wife. I have a right to know when you get paid and how much."

Steve struck her on the mouth several times. "I'll show you how much right you have to meddle in my affairs. You needn't cry either. What else did you take out of my wallet?"

"I took nothing that belongs to you. I had to take the things from the pockets to wash your clothes."

"Next time leave my clothes on me. Don't go looking for excuses to go through my pockets."

"See that there is not a next time."

Steve struck her again.

The next morning Nancy's face was swollen so badly from Steve's blows that she didn't go to work.

In the afternoon Nancy answered a rap at the door. "Does a T. Steven Stank—— something live here?"

"Yes."

"We got a desk to deliver here."

"A desk? Are you sure?"

"I ain't crazy, lady."

"Perhaps I am."

The two men brought a large roll-top desk up the stairs. It was a struggle to get it into the apartment.

That evening while they were eating supper, Nancy asked, "Did you buy a desk, Steve?"

"Yes, did they deliver it."

"It's in the living room. It looks very nice under the clock."

Steve went into the living room. "Come here,

Nancy,"

"Yes?" She stood beside him.

Fiercely he turned to her. "This is my desk for my things. Don't ever touch it, or don't ever let anyone else touch it. Do you understand?"

"Yes." Nancy turned into the kitchen to finish the dishes.

# CHAPTER 11

The rent money was gone. Nancy searched her purse and looked on the floor. "I'll go upstairs and look. I must have dropped it when I got something else from my purse." Doctor Randall's patients were all gone from the waiting room. Mrs. Randall was cleaning the offices and waiting room.

Upstairs Nancy conducted a fruitless search of the entire apartment.

"I'm sorry," she told the dentist's wife shame-facedly, "someone must have taken it."

"Don't you lock your door?"

"Yes. Perhaps at work. . . ."

"But Mrs. Way employs only trustworthy people, does she not?"

"Yes." Slowly a seed of doubt crept into her mind. *Where did Steve get the money to purchase the desk?* "I must have been careless and dropped it when I got something else from my purse," said Nancy quickly.

"I'll wait until next weeek," Mrs. Randall told her kindly.

"Would you let me clean the offices again?"

"That won't be necessary. I'm sure you'll pay when you can."

However, knowing how hard it would be to make it up, Nancy insisted. She cleaned the offices three evenings a week after she was through working at the café.

Nancy thought it wise not to mention the rent money. Steve spent many evenings in front of his desk. Even some Saturday evenings in the next few weeks Steve sat in front of the desk before he went out for the night.

Nancy detested the liquor odor that often hung heavy about Steve. Saturday night and Sunday were bad days for Nancy.

Bill came home from business school on a wet Saturday. Steve was already gone for the evening when Bill stopped in to see his sister.

"Hello, sister," he greeted her cordially. "Smells like supper."

"Want to stay?"

"Thanks, but Mother is expecting me. I just wanted to tell you I'm going to be proprietor of Harris's grocery store. Mrs. Harris is ill, and her husband wants to be home with her. I can pay him little by little until I have it all paid. I had a small down payment." Bill's eyes shone with joy.

"You certainly are fortunate." A note of bitterness crept into Nancy's voice.

"But, Nancy," Bill's happiness clouded, "I've

worked hard toward this and prayed."

"I know, but my hard work seems to get me nowhere."

Bill left abruptly.

Nancy felt mean because she had spoken so sharply to her brother. Soon tears of self-pity ran as fast as the rain against the windowpane.

Sunday was a gloomy day with Steve once again sleeping off the effects of liquor. It was no use to cook a nice meal, so Nancy ate nothing.

Monday morning Nancy awoke early with the sun shining in her face. Slowly she dressed. When she was almost ready for work, Steve came into the kitchen.

"I'm going to Mason City on business," he told her curtly.

Angrily Nancy faced him. "If you'd told me sooner, I could have gotten a day off and gone with you. I could do with a day off too."

"I didn't ask you to go along." Monday was never a day to argue with Steve. "Give me money for the bus fare."

"I don't have money for you. I'm not your slave." She slammed the door behind her. She had taken one step down toward the street when Steve caught her and dragged her back into the apartment. He pushed her into a chair. "Now give me the money."

When Nancy sat without moving he snatched her purse and helped himself to all the money she had in it.

Enraged she went to work.

"Did you swallow some nettles?" asked Mrs. Way when she came in. Nancy did not answer.

During the morning Nancy broke a cup, spilling coffee on a tablecloth. Nothing seemed to go right. By noon she was tired and weak, and her mood matched the ache of her body. While washing dishes, she broke a glass and cut her hand.

"That's a deep cut, Nancy," said Mrs. Way sympathetically. "You had better see a doctor. It needs stitches."

"I'll make out if I can keep my hand out of water a few days," she said tartly. "I'll do double share of dishwashing when it's healed."

"Well, I ought not allow it," said her employer slowly.

"I can't afford a doctor," snapped Nancy.

Mrs. Way shrugged and let it pass. Linnea, the counter girl, wrapped the cut and offered to trade places with her. "I'll do your share of dishwashing for a couple of days." She patted Nancy's shoulder kindly. Tears filled Nancy's eyes. She hurried to the washroom to compose and tidy herself.

When Nancy returned to the counter, Harvey was there for his chat and cup of coffee.

"Did Steve quit Johnson's crew, Nancy?"

"No," she said shortly.

"Well, just wondered. You needn't bite my head off. I saw him hitchhiking west of town early this morning. Just figured he was leaving town."

Nancy turned her back. *Steve hitchhiking?* She didn't want Harvey to see her surprise. Quickly she spoke, "He had business in Mason City. Is that any of your business?"

"Nancy isn't feeling well." Linnea leaped to the role of peacemaker. It would never do to provoke Harvey. "She cut her hand badly."

"I'm sorry, Nancy. You look kind of sick."

"It's the weather," Nancy managed to smile.

\* \* \*

Steve came home Wednesday evening.

"Did you eat supper?" she asked, not too cordially.

"No."

Nancy heated soup and made a sandwich for him. "You'll have to wash your own dish. I cut my hand."

"Is this all I get as a welcome home?"

"That's all the food I have. You took all my money."

"Now that your brother owns a grocery store you ought to be able to get credit."

"I won't ask my family to give us anything," retorted Nancy. "Anyway, how did I know you were coming back tonight? They told me you left town hitchhiking. How did I know if you were ever coming back?"

"I won't leave until the harvest is over," Steve told her.

"You mean you're going with the crew again."

"You're the biggest fussbudget I ever knew. Of course I'm going with the crew."

There were some good days, and there were days Nancy wished the crew would leave real soon.

One Saturday it was apparent that Mr. Johnson's crew was leaving Dry Forks.

"Is Steve deserting you again?" Mrs. Way asked.

"He's going with the harvest crew."

That night Nancy felt as though she had just dropped off to sleep when she was awakened by a noise.

She reached for the light switch. It was 3:00 a.m. The knock on the door sounded again. Then a voice hollered, "It's Iky. Come on down and help Steve home."

Nancy quickly dressed and went with Iky. She had never been in a bar before.

"There ought to be a law against all liquor sale," declared Nancy as she coaxed Steve to come with her.

Out on the sidewalk at last, Steve staggered and leaned heavily on her. Then he fell to the sidewalk. No matter how much she tried she could not move him or get him to move.

Nancy could hardly bring herself to ask anyone to help her. At last she walked to her home. Bill did not scold. He helped her to take Steve home and get him on the bed.

Bill started to help Steve out of his clothes.

"Don't, Bill. Just leave him alone."

"It's awfully hot, and his clothes stink."

"I know, but he gets angry if you take his clothes off. He thinks someone else took his money then."

"Just as you say." He looked at her anxiously. "Will you be all right?"

Bill sat on the sofa, and Nancy dozed in her chair. At last he went into the kitchen and made scrambled eggs and coffee. They ate in silence.

"I'll soon have to go to church, Nancy."

"This is by no means the first time I've been alone with Steve when he was drunk. That's not as bad as afterward."

"I'd urge you to go home with me, but your place is with your husband."

"I know," cried Nancy. "Pray for me."

"Sally and I have special prayer for you and Steve every Sunday night."

"You do?" She was often surprised at her brother's deep Christian way of life.

"I'd like to tell you a secret."

"Go on and tell it."

"Sally and I are to be married on Christmas Eve."

"Oh, Bill, I'm so glad for you."

"We thought if I do the work, I could close part of the back porch off Mother's bedroom. That way she could be alone some and we would be close by." He stood ready to go.

"Bill," Nancy paused as though she would not go on, and then, "I think I'll go to church today. Maybe if I set a Christian example, I can win

Steve. I'll feel better anyway if I get right with the Lord again."

"We've prayed for the day when you'd come to church again."

If Dry Forks Chapel members were surprised to see Nancy at church, they gave no indication of it. Everyone greeted her as though it was only last Sunday that she had been at church.

That evening Steve cried when he learned that he had once again failed to go with the harvest crew.

# CHAPTER 12

"That's a pretty sight," Steve indicated the large rolling wheat field they were walking past.

"You like wheat?" Nancy spoke softly, remembering.

"Especially ripened wheat," said Steve. "Ripened wheat means work for me."

"Why do you like to work in wheat harvesting?"

"That's a silly question. Why do you like waitress work rather than ironing or cleaning?"

"I like to meet people," said Nancy thoughtfully.

"Yes," laughed her husband, "and look who you met seven years ago."

Nancy was silent.

"Are you glad you were working in the café

seven years ago?" Steve asked at last.

"Now you're asking silly questions." Nancy tried not to think of the sad times she'd had since she met Steve. The past year had been too wonderful. Nancy sighed.

"Why the big sigh?"

"My feet ache."

"Perhaps we shouldn't have walked out to church this evening."

"I should be used to walking those two miles," Nancy smiled contentedly. "It seems like only half the distance since you walk with me."

"Maybe we should buy a car."

"I don't mind walking to church. I'd rather save toward buying a little place."

Steve unlocked the door to their apartment, and they went upstairs.

"Seems so warm for May." He was opening the windows, but Nancy had already sought the comfort of the rocker.

Steve looked at her. "You sick?"

"Just tired."

"Your feet surely are swollen. I'll get some warm water to soak them."

Steve whistled snatches of "Sweet Hour of Prayer" while he drew the water and set it on the stove to heat. "Guess I'll get ready for bed while I wait. Tomorrow's a big day. Comptons want six cabins finished before the harvest crews come."

When Steve set the pail of warm water in front of Nancy, she was asleep. He touched her flushed face. "You are sick. Maybe you'd better stay home from work tomorrow."

Nancy was sick in bed almost a week.

"You had better take another week to rest," Doctor Braddock told her on Friday. "This summer grippe leaves the body weak, and your blood pressure is low. Take long walks and rest a lot."

On Monday morning Nancy walked to the grocery store. "Good morning, Bill."

"Say, you're out bright and early," greeted her brother from behind the counter. "What can I get for you?"

"Something Mother especially likes. Steve went to Mason City on business. I'm going to spend the day with Mother."

"Mom doesn't fry chicken anymore. Thinks it's too much bother for just one person, and she doesn't come over on our side of the house to eat anymore. She says she doesn't want to butt into our family life too much."

"I guess as people get older they like a little quiet too."

"Are you implying that our twins are noisy?" laughed Bill. "Girls aren't noisy."

"Ruth and Rhoda are bursting with energy though," said Nancy. "Give me a nice frying chicken. Big enough so that Sally and the girls can share with us too. You don't go home for dinner, do you?"

"No, I eat here. One of these days I will have to hire help. Sally can't help much anymore."

"I'll be seeing you," called Nancy over her

shoulder as she left the store with her purchases.

The morning slipped by swiftly. "Smells delicious," said Sally as she helped to set the food on the table. "It was kind of you to share your meal with us, Nancy. I got all my clothes on the line because I didn't have to stop and fix dinner."

"Me want a drumstick," yelled Ruth.

"Me want drumstick," chimed in Rhoda. The three-year-old girls were like two dynamos. They ate quietly for a while.

"Ruth want cake," fretted the sandy-haired girl.

"Cake! Cake!" They shouted.

"You'll have to finish your vegetables," their mother told them.

"No! No! No!" they whimpered.

"I know a remedy for cranky girls," said Sally firmly. She washed the sticky little fingers and took them upstairs.

*　*　*

"Mother, what did you do with the things that were in my closet?" asked Nancy as they washed the dishes together.

"There wasn't much left. A few old dresses that I knew you didn't want. I crocheted the good parts into that rug I gave you for Christmas. The rest of the things Sally boxed up and put in the closet under the stairs."

"I thought perhaps I could find my knitting bag and knit something nice for Sally's new baby

71

with that leftover yarn."

"She'd appreciate that. She gave some of the twins' tiny things to Mrs. Dutton and some to her sister. Her sister needs them again this year."

"The wee ones are asleep already," said Sally as she entered the kitchen.

"I was wishing for my knitting bag."

"I'll get it for you."

Nancy hurried home at four-thirty, eager to knit once again.

"Knit six; purl one; knit across; yarn over." The little book, *Pretty Things for Baby*, lay open on her lap.

"Purl six; knit one. . . ."

A horn on the street frightened Nancy. "I must have been asleep. Eleven o'clock. Maybe Steve won't be home tonight. It's quite a trip. Perhaps he couldn't make bus connections. I may as well go to bed."

The next morning Nancy was eager to knit again, but she decided to follow the doctor's instructions and take a walk first. After lunch she took a short nap and then took her knitting downstairs into the tiny backyard.

*I wish Steve wouldn't be so closemouthed when he takes a trip to Mason City,* Nancy reflected as she prepared for bed. *About once a year—I always thought he just went for a drinking party. Maybe. . . .*

*No, Steve's a Christian now, and I'll have faith in him.* A tear stole down her cheek. *See here,* she told her reflection in the mirror. *If Steve had been hurt, I would have heard.* She opened her Bible and read before she knelt to pray for his safe return.

Late that night Steve crept quietly into the apartment.

"Steve?" called Nancy.

"Yes. Just go back to sleep. I'll sleep on the sofa so as not to disturb you."

"Did you have a good trip? Have you had supper?"

"Yes. Yes. Go back to sleep."

At the breakfast table Nancy furtively looked at Steve. He looked haggard and needed a shave. "Did you get the special nails you needed?" she inquired.

When Steve did not answer, she repeated her question.

"Yes, don't ask so many questions," grumbled Steve. "I have a headache."

"But where are the nails?"

"I couldn't carry a bunch of nails on a bus. I just ordered them."

"Couldn't the lumberyard have ordered them for you?"

"Don't ask so many questions," he shouted. "I told you I don't feel good."

"Steve!" Nancy shrank back. "I was only— only trying to—to—"

"Leave me alone." He left for work.

"He left his lunch," said Nancy to her empty kitchen. "If I didn't know better, I'd think he had

73

been drinking. Oh! No! He can't start that again," cried Nancy. "I must quit being suspicious." Nevertheless, her day was clouded, and she prayed more earnestly that Steve would remain true to his Christian vow.

# CHAPTER 13

A man entered the café as Nancy was starting the morning coffee.

"Where can I find Steve?"

*Where have I heard that voice before*, she wondered as she eyed him cautiously.

"You're out early in the morning," she hedged.

"Have to be. We expect a big harvest this year."

"You're a bit early for that."

"Not much. Wheat's ready to cut south a mile. A crew boss has to scout for muscle early. Where did you say I could find Steve?"

"He isn't able to work in the harvest this year." She just couldn't let Steve get involved in a harvest crew that drank, and she assumed all of them did drink liquor.

"Is he sick?"

"He isn't getting any younger."

"Come now, Nancy, you know Steve is ageless."

"He has a good job."

Just then Mrs. Way came from the kitchen. "Well, well, look who's here. Nancy, have you gotten his order?"

Nancy poised with her pencil ready to write.

"Bacon, scrambled eggs, coffee, and toast."

After the customer had eaten and left, Mrs. Way asked, "How come you were so friendly with a customer, Nancy?" Even though she laughed when she asked the question, Nancy flushed.

"He was asking for Steve, and I was glad you came in when you did. I didn't want to tell him where to find Steve. Steve has a good job."

The apartment was hot when Nancy came home from work. She opened the windows and kicked off her shoes.

"Guess I'll rest a bit."

Steve's footsteps awakened her. "I didn't mean to fall asleep." She hurried about to get their supper.

The meal was eaten in silence. Nancy interpreted Steve's silence to be an expression of displeasure because supper was late.

"I'm sorry I fell asleep and didn't have supper cooked."

"That's better than if you'd fallen asleep while it was cooking and burned it."

Steve walked about the apartment restlessly. Finally he spoke. "How come you wouldn't tell Con Ebbling where I was working?"

"I don't even know Con Ebbling."

"You know that a man came looking for me."

"Steve," she cried, "you can't go and work for him."

"Who says I can't?"

"You have a good job as a carpenter."

"After harvest I can take up where I left off. Compton's cabins are finished, all but a little trim."

"Millers want their porch fixed," argued Nancy.

"That can wait till after harvest. Con Ebbling will give me twenty-five cents an hour more this year. I've always worked in harvest, and I'm going to again."

"For the past five years you've been going north with the crew and been too drunk to make it out of here when they left. You know all harvesters drink—"

"So you don't trust me," said Steve angrily.

"Yes, but . . . but. . . ." Too late Nancy realized that she had said the wrong thing.

Steve started working in the harvest fields on Monday. Harvesters meant hard work for Nancy also. Mrs. Way raised her pay.

Steve worked until eight o'clock on week nights. On Saturday night they quit at six o'clock.

It was eight-thirty the first Saturday night before Nancy heard his footsteps on the stairs. There was no mistaking the odor he brought with him. A wave of nausea swept over her.

"Steve," she whispered, "you have been drinking."

"I wish you'd try to understand, Nancy. A little drink is good for anyone. The Bible even says you can drink for your stomach's sake."

"What's wrong with your stomach?"

"Quit nagging. Ebbling bought the drinks for the whole crew. I'm not going to be a sissy and say no. But you don't understand."

"I do understand. That is just why I didn't want you to work around those drinking men, but you wouldn't listen to me."

"You aren't my boss," shouted Steve. "Get that straight."

"I know, Steve." Nancy tried to keep calm. "I was only suggesting that you stay away from temptation."

"Let's eat supper."

\* \* \*

Weeks seemed to drag. It was a miracle that Steve drank only a little while working with Con Ebbling's crew. *If only he holds out until they're gone and gets back to his carpentering,* Nancy thought.

"I must be getting old," Nancy told Steve one evening. "These long days in the café while the harvest crews are here just about get me down."

"There's at least two weeks of cutting in these parts."

Those two weeks seemed like two months to Nancy, but at last the Friday came when some of the harvest crews left Dry Forks. Saturday more left.

The café was crowded on Saturday noon. "We came in for one of your good meals before we leave," one of the crew bosses laughingly told Mrs. Way.

"Sure is good pie," said another.

"Nancy bakes all my pies. She's my best waitress." Mrs. Way looked around but couldn't locate Nancy with her eyes. "She must have gone to the kitchen."

Linnea was beckoning to Mrs. Way from the kitchen door.

"What is it, Linnea?"

"Nancy's sick. She fainted in the washroom!"

Mrs. Way was already on her way to the back of the café.

"I'm all right now," Nancy said weakly. "It's just that it's so hot."

"All the men are served. There won't be much doing because both these crews are leaving. Do you think you can make it home alone?"

"I'm sure I can and thanks."

At home Nancy took off her uniform and dropped on the bed.

The room was dark when she awoke. She found the light switch and turned it on. The alarm clock said eight o'clock.

"I can't go to the store. I forgot to get my pay envelope. Soup will be fine. Steve had a big meal at noon at the café."

Supper was ready. Nancy sat on her rocker and began to knit.

"There we are. Finished at last." She held up the tiny white sweater.

"I'll have to eat my soup alone," she said as she went into the kitchen. "Nine o'clock. Temptation must have gotten the best of him at last."

Nancy sat on her rocker and read her Bible. It was hard to settle down. She went and lay on the bed. "Steve will probably be too drunk to make it home alone. It's no use to undress," she sighed.

"Oh, God," she sobbed as morning light crept over Dry Forks, "help me not to hate Con Ebbling. It was so wonderful before he came and coaxed Steve to work for him."

Her tears were all spent. She didn't feel well at all. *No one would feel well after crying as much as I have,* she thought, *but I just can't help it.*

Sunday morning was long at home alone. She looked at the clock when she noticed the neighbors coming home from church. "Twelve o'clock. I can't eat anything." She poured a glass of milk and drank half of it.

Late in the afternoon there was a knock on the door. She flew to open the door.

"Oh, Bill."

"You don't sound glad to see me," laughed her brother.

Nancy stood looking out of the window.

"Someone in the store last evening said that you had gone home from work sick. When neither you nor Steve were in church this morning, I thought I'd better check."

Nancy swallowed hard but could find no words to answer.

"What's wrong, Sis?"

"I hate him! I hate him!" cried Nancy. "He took Steve."

"Nancy! Stop crying and tell me! Where is Steve?"

"I don't know. I don't know. He must have gone with the harvest crew without even telling me. It's all Con Ebblng's fault."

Bill sat with Nancy a long while. Only Nancy's dry hollow sobs filled the quietness.

At last Bill spoke. "Come home with me."

"No. Maybe I'm wrong. There's not much chance, but if Steve should come back, I ought to be here. Thanks for coming. It has helped to talk to you."

Bill blew his nose. "I—I—we'll pray for you."

# CHAPTER 14

"I'm really not sick," Nancy told her mother who had walked four blocks to visit her.

"You don't look well," said her mother.

"I'm all right. It's just that—" she caught her breath.

"I didn't come to pry."

"I know." It was no use. Tears fell like a summer shower.

"Steve hasn't come back?" Mrs. Yoder asked softly.

Nancy only sobbed and shook her head negatively.

"I'm sorry, Nancy." Her mother broke into sobbing at last. "There seems to be so little I can say to comfort you."

"It makes me feel better just to have you here, Mother."

"Then I'll come often."

"Two days of crying is enough. It doesn't do any good. I'm going back to work tomorrow."

"Why there goes Linnea home from work. I must be getting home."

Wednesday afternoon Linnea and Nancy walked home from work in the hot August sunshine. Nancy was going to the grocery store.

As they walked by Nancy's street door, she noticed a letter in her letter slot. "I don't often get mail. I'll see what it is. You may as well go on without me."

Nancy snatched the letter and ran up the stairs. It was postmarked Montana. She ran a table knife under the flap. A small piece of paper fluttered to the floor.

Steve's poor handwriting scrawled across the paper.

"I owe Con Ebbling too much. I had to go. I could not say good-bye."

She didn't know whether to laugh or to cry.

"What does he owe Con Ebbling?" Nancy asked herself bitterly. "Perhaps for a drink."

81

The days for Nancy were much the same. She arose early, worked in the café, did the housework, and dropped into bed only to toss and think how life might have been.

One September evening Nancy rushed home from work. Taking a nicely-wrapped package from her bureau drawer, she made her way to her former home.

The front door was closed against the heat of the day. The house was strangely quiet for Bill's home. She rapped on the door.

A stranger opened the door.

"Good afternoon. I'm Mrs. Yoder's sister-in-law. Is she allowed to have visitors?"

"Come on in," called Sally from the bedroom. "I'm not ill."

"You are looking spry and happy," said Nancy, stepping into the bedroom.

"Isn't it wonderful?" bubbled Sally. "Meet Rebecca." She pointed to the neatly padded clothes basket on the chest at the foot of the bed.

"So you named my new niece Rebecca." Nancy lifted the cover from the tiny bundle. "She's a fat little mite."

"And ever so sweet."

"Wasn't Bill disappointed that she wasn't a boy?"

"No," laughed Sally. "The baby is healthy."

"I brought a little gift." She handed the package to Sally.

"Oh, Nancy." Sally held up the tiny white sweater. "It's so soft. It will keep Becky warm this winter. Thank you so much."

"There was only enough yarn left for a sweater."

"Oh, this was your baby's yarn," said Sally softly. "I never thought I'd—I'd use the yarn for my baby."

"There's no one I'd rather see have it and maybe—would you—Babies don't wear out a little sweater."

"You'd like to have it back when I'm through with it. Sure. Don't be shy about asking. My sisters and I do that all the time."

Suddenly realization dawned on Sally.

"Oh, Nancy!"

Too late Nancy turned her back. She should not let Sally see tears. "I hope Steve comes back before March. Pray that he will, Sally."

"We'll all pray."

"I want him so badly."

"I know." She shook her head sadly. "A woman needs her man at a time like that. Steve didn't. . . ."

"No—He has his weak points but he didn't know. He didn't desert me because of it or to escape the financial part. Anyway there is enough in the bank to care for the baby and me even if I have to quit working soon. If I could engage the girl you have instead of going clear to Sylvan Springs to the hospital, it wouldn't be nearly as expensive."

"You'd better ask her now," whispered Sally. "She's booked up way ahead."

*　　*　　*

The weather was cooling off. *I had better go
back to the café for my sweater. October is too
changeable not to have it in the morning when I
go to work.* She turned and almost ran into a
man.

"Excuse me. I didn't know there was anyone
behind me."

When she came out of the café with her
sweater, he was standing beide the door. Nancy
stopped. The man said nothing. Slowly she
walked down the street with the man following
her. She did not want him to follow her all the
way home. She turned and faced the stranger.
"Are you looking for someone?"

"He tell me she work in café. You know Tag
Stankiewiez's wife?"

"What do you want with her?" she held her
sweater tight to still her trembling hands.

"I want to speak to her."

"What about?"

"You know her?"

"Yes." Nancy was agitated. "What do you
want?"

"I haff businez."

"What kind of business?"

"I find her first."

"Do you know where Steve is?"

"Steve?"

"We call Mr. Stankiewiez, Steve."

"Ho! Ho! Ho! Steve it is in thee's town."

84

"What do you want?"

"If you give me money I tell where Steve is, Nancy."

Fear caught at Nancy. The man even knew her name. *How long had he been following her unnoticed?*

"Is Steve in trouble?"

"You no vant ever'one to hear," the dark-skinned man indicated the people walking on the sidewalk. "Ve go to your house."

"We can talk here." People were looking at her as they passed. What should she do? "What are you after?"

"Your man no come back if you no pay me the debt."

"Debt! What debt?"

"Ve gamble. I vin. Tag owe me money."

"How much money?"

"He owe me tree hunnerd dollar."

"Three hundred dollars!"

"I vill settle for two."

"You mean you want me to give you two hundred dollars?"

"You katch on kweek."

"But I can't."

"You no see your man again. I'm tired vaiting for me money."

Nancy thought of the money with which they had meant to buy a little place. Steve and she had even looked at a few.

"I don't have that much money *for you*."

"How much?"

85

*What can I do? God, help me to do the right thing.*

"Meet me here tomorrow at this time. I'll see what I can do."

"Come," he pointed to Iky's. "I get you a dreenk."

"I don't drink," she retorted.

"Ha, ha, ha. Tag say hees vife is Christian. She no dreenk." His laughter followed her up Easly Street. She ducked into the alley and went to the grocery store.

At six o'clock Nancy knocked at her mother's door.

"Is supper ready?" she tried to sound cheerful.

"Almost. Are you going to stay?" Her mother was already reaching into the cupboard for another plate.

"I'm—I'm not feeling so well. I get blue when I'm alone so much."

"You come any time you want to." Mrs. Yoder bustled about.

Nancy ate more heartily than she had for some time. It did help to have companionship.

"Did you tell Mrs. Way you are planning to quit work?"

"Yes. She wants me to bake pies at home. That way I can keep on after the baby is here."

"That would be nice."

The next morning Harvey came in for his chat. There was a lull in business at the café.

"I'd like to go to the bank if you don't mind, Mrs. Way."

"Silly. When did I ever refuse to allow my girls to go to the bank? Not too often they go between paydays though." Laughingly she winked at Harvey.

"Cash or check?" asked the girl behind the wicket at the bank.

Nancy hesitated. She hadn't thought of this. "Cash."

After the girl was gone a long time Mr. Heere, the bank president, came to the front of the bank. "Will you come into my office, Nancy?"

"Is something wrong, Mr. Heere?"

"You asked to draw some money out of your savings account?"

"Isn't that my privilege," she responded. "I didn't know there were strings attached."

"No, no, but—Nancy. . . ." Mr. Heere ran his fingers around his collar as though it were too tight and finally opened it. "Nancy, I. . . ."

"What's the matter?" she asked fearfully.

"You—you—don't have any money in your savings account."

"I—I—What? What do you mean?"

"There isn't any savings account."

"But Mr. Heere, we had almost a thousand dollars in our savings account."

"There isn't any now."

"How could that be?"

"I—I—Steve. . . ."

"You mean Steve took it out?"

"I thought you knew about it. He said you wanted to buy a little place."

"Steve took all our money?" She spoke as though in a daze. "But the man wants two hundred dollars."

"What man?" asked Mr. Heere. Tears welled up and spilled over as she told the fatherly old man about the threat of the man.

"I'll meet him and put a stop to his game," said Mr. Heere.


# CHAPTER 15

"Are we finished?" Nancy looked about the kitchen, her hands deep in the hot, sudsy water.

"Here's one pie pan and a fork," replied her mother.

"I think we'll close up the bake business for today. Four o'clock. Not bad. It took me until eight or nine o'clock to make Mrs. Way's Saturday order at first."

"I'm afraid it will take me that long when I take over." Mrs. Yoder was staying with Nancy as the time neared for Nancy's baby to be born.

"You sit down, Mother. I'm going to scrub the kitchen floor before I join you."

Mrs. Yoder was sitting on the sofa dozing when Nancy entered the living room.

"That's done." Nancy took off her apron and sat on the rocker. "Feels good to sit down for a spell."

"I'm going to finish patching this trouser leg of

Bill's, if you don't mind," she reached for her thimble.

"I don't mind," yawned Nancy, "as long as I don't have to do it. All I want to do is sit here and enjoy looking at my nicely-scrubbed kitchen floor."

"Will that be too much breeze for you, Mother?"

"No, it's been warm all week. March isn't usually this warm."

"I thought the floor would dry more quickly with a little breeze."

The click of the needle against the thimble lulled Nancy to sleep. She woke when her mother got up and closed the window.

"I must have slept a long time." It was hard to see one another in the gathering gloom.

"About ten minutes. There seems to be a dust storm under way."

"Oh, no, not one of those March dust storms just when I washed my kitchen floor so nicely."

Nancy shivered at the *grit-grit* of her feet on the dusty floor. The wind howled.

"Maybe if we wait a while," suggested Nancy, "we can get supper without seasoning it with grit."

"I've seen a few such storms last six or eight hours." Her mother was looking out the front window. "It's a bad one. I can scarcely see across the street."

"I'd better start a fire. It's getting chilly." Nancy got her coat from the closet, then sat down on a kitchen chair.

"Would you please get the kindling, Mother?"

Mrs. Yoder looked at her and then hurried downstairs to the shed in which the wood was kept.

\* \* \*

"Too bad to get you out on a night like this, Doctor Braddock," Bill apologized.

"That's what I'm here for."

Bill and the doctor hurried through the swirling sand to Nancy's apartment.

Then Bill left to get the girl that had helped them when Becky was born. She lived fifteen miles west of Dry Forks on a farm.

The blowing sand made it difficult to see. The car headlights hardly penetrated the dust screen.

Bill shivered. "Terrible night to be out," he muttered to himself. He inched the car along the highway. "No one else out tonight." The tires went *swish* and sand growled and gritted as Bill's car moved through the drifts of sand.

His eyes were tired of trying to see. "My turn-off should be here somewhere." He glanced at his speedometer. "I've come a mile since the six-mile road." He pulled to the right and stopped. "I hope I'm off the road in case someone else is out. Can't seem to see the edge of the macadam."

In spite of the cold wind that tore at the car, Bill wiped perspiration from his face. "There we are. Only the tops of the fence posts showing." Carefully he maneuvered the car between the two fences. "If I would have known it was this bad, I could have waited until morning."

"Three more miles."

Suddenly the car engine died. "I was afraid of that. I can feel the electricity in the air."

Grit filled his mouth; his eyes felt sore, and his shoes were heavy with sand when he finally reached the Engle farm. His repeated knocks on the door seemed to be caught up in the roaring wind. Finally he opened the door and went inside.

"Hullo," he called.

"Who's there," came a voice from deep within.

"Bill Yoder. My sister needs Elvira. My car quit three miles back. I'll need a chain."

Portly Mrs. Engle entered the kitchen. "I'll get the fire 'drawed up' while you hitch up. Pa, this man's near froze. He needs to be warmed up 'fore he starts back."

One! Two! Three! Four! The clock on the mantel struck.

"Is that clock right time?"

"Yes, 'tis, Mr. Yoder."

"No wonder I'm tired. It took me four hours to get here."

Ma Engle put her head inside the stair door and called, "Viry, you got a customer down here."

"I'm about ready, Ma."

"Here." Ma set a plate of fried eggs, two slices

91

of toast, and a cup of steaming coffee before him.

Elvira had just joined him at the table as her father stepped inside. "The rig's at the front gate."

Pa Engle took the plate his wife offered him and sat down.

"No use to wash my hands. The eggs are gritty anyway."

Silverware clinked on their plates. Ma's feet ground out a tune across the gritty floor as she served more eggs, bread, and coffee.

At last Pa scraped his chair back and shrugged into his heavy coat which had hung on a hook above his head at the table.

"I'll see you in three weeks, Ma." Elvira told her mother.

Bill climbed on the wagon seat and the girl snuggled under a buffalo robe on the back of the wagon.

"The horses know the way," said Pa. Conversation was impossible above the roar of the wind.

The horses stopped. "Now what?" asked Bill.

"There's your car, no?"

"That was a short ride compared to my trip in to your house."

Pa jumped down from the wagon and fastened the chain on the back bumper of Bill's car. Elvira settled herself inside the car.

"That chain ought to take care of the static electricity," hollered Mr. Engle. "Jump in and see if she'll start."

The starter growled and the motor came alive.

"I'll bring your chain home as soon as the storm's over," shouted Bill.

"Bring it home with Viry. That's soon enough."

"I never knew a car was able to crawl so slowly," offered Elvira after they'd been buffeting sand drifts for an hour.

"Not too often I travel this slow."

"Do you see stars?" she asked at last.

"Yes," growled Bill. "There's stars floating all over the windshield when you stare into the swirl any length of time. Guess I'll have to stop and rest my eyes."

It was eight o'clock before Elvira Engle and Bill crunched their way up the stairs to Nancy's apartment.

"You look worn out, son." His mother greeted them with the crying baby in her arms.

"David has been here four hours already," called Nancy from her bedroom.

"Sounds like he can almost outdo the wind for howling," teased Bill. "You ought to call him Sandy. I wonder if I'll ever get the sand out of my system."

"Or the house," added Nancy as she looked beside the bed at her usually brightly flowered linoleum. Not a red or yellow rose shone through the grit on the floor.

Later that week Elvira approached Nancy, "I guess I'll have to dry the little man's diapers in the living room. It wouldn't do any good to hang them out."

"No, it wouldn't," sighed Nancy.

"The clean ones are just about all gone."

"I didn't prepare enough diapers for three days of dust storm."

"Humph," snorted Miss Engle that evening as she folded the grit-yellowed diapers. "I set great store by the white diapers I hang on a line when I'm nursing at a place."

"Don't feel so badly, Elvira," said Nancy. "Those weren't hanging on a line. You dried them on a wooden rack."

They both laughed and felt a little more relaxed.

Next morning Elvira woke with a start. Something was wrong.

"What's wrong?" asked Nancy frightened.

Sunshine was streaming in the window. Miss Engle laughed, "Nothing's wrong. The wind has quit."

"And that big boy didn't wake up all night."

Miss Engle set to work sweeping grit, shoveling it into a bucket and carrying it out. There wasn't a corner that didn't get touched.

# CHAPTER 16

Nancy counted sixty dollars from her treasure chest.

"Bill just drove up in front." Elvira Engle held her purse and suitcase in her hand. Nancy handed her the money.

"I charge fifty dollars for three weeks of service." Miss Engle handed a ten-dollar bill back to Nancy.

"You worked extra hard cleaning up the grit."

"That's not your fault there was a dust storm. Now take it back. I don't want to keep your brother waiting. Good-bye and God bless you. I enjoyed my three weeks here."

Nancy sank back on her rocker with the baby in her arms. "I have no reason to be glad Miss Engle is gone, Davie," crooned Nancy softly, "but it will be so good to have you all to myself. I'd gladly share you with your daddy though." She did not realize she was crying until a tear dropped on the baby's cheek.

"I must not wet you down with tears, but I can't raise you alone and yet. . . ." A groan escaped her lips. "I pray you will never see him drunk. Would it be better to be alone . . . or? . . ."

Nancy laid the baby on the sofa and sank to her knees beside him.

"Dear Father," she sobbed, "here is my baby. Help me to teach him to be good and grow up to work for Thee. When Steve comes back, help me to live a Christian example before him so he won't drink again."

\* \* \*

David was six weeks old.

"Every Sunday, unless we're sick we are going

to church," she told the baby as she tucked him into the soft white sweater and tied his cap strings under his chin. She was rewarded with a big smile. Bill was waiting in the car to take them to church. It was a full day. They stayed at her mother's for dinner. It was bedtime when her brother brought them home.

Monday was washday for Nancy. Tuesday she baked for Mrs. Way. On Wednesday she baked rolls and pies for the new Dry Forks House Hotel.

"Thursday again," Nancy yawned. "We'll have to hurry, David, I overslept and Mrs. Way wants sixteen pies today."

She scarcely took time to eat lunch. At last the baby was in bed for his afternoon nap.

"There, these pies can cool, and I'll run down to the backyard and get David's diapers off the line."

"I'm glad I consented to let Bill deliver the pies with the car after the store closes. I can't haul much baked goods on the wagon with David in it. It means so many trips and I am tired."

Nancy was deep in thought and did not see the man at her door until she was almost against him.

"Are you looking for—Steve!"

They just stared at each other.

"Well, let's go on in the house."

"This is a nice surprise. You're a bit early for harvest. How did you get into town?"

"Hitchhiked."

"You look ill. Are you?"

"Not exactly. I—I just have a sore hand and feel kind of queer."

"Let's have a look at it."

Steve held out a badly swollen hand. In the center was a small puncture wound.

"What happened, Steve?"

There was no answer for a long time. He looked as though he were trying to think of what did happen. "It's no good trying to lie to you. I was drinking and got in a fight. A fellow stuck a knife in it."

Steve looked so thin and haggard that Nancy felt sorry for him. "Come and soak it in warm salt water. That is Mother's favorite remedy for sores like that."

Nancy poured a basin of water, added salt, and pulled it to the back of the stove. Pulling a stool beside it, Steve sat down and soaked his hand.

"That sure feels good," he said after a time.

"Steve," Nancy hesitated, "you looked so ill that I didn't want to spring a surprise on you too quickly, but I do have a nice surprise."

Steve looked at her and waited. "Well, go ahead and spring it."

"We have a six-week-old son."

Steve stared at Nancy.

"He's a very good baby," she said at last.

"Can you put some salve on this hand?"

Nancy put ointment on the hand and wrapped it with a strip of an old sheet.

"Just like the Good Samaritan," sighed Steve.

"Take these aspirins and lie down for a nap."

Willingly he followed her orders.

Two hours passed by. Steve was still asleep when David awoke. After a time Nancy was aware of being watched as she sat rocking the baby. Steve just stood in the doorway of the bedroom.

"Come and join us." Nancy moved to the sofa, and Steve sat beside her. "Say hello to your son."

"He looks like me, doesn't he?"

"Very much so."

The evening meal was a pleasant one. Steve told Nancy a few things that happened while he was traveling with the harvest crew. The baby whimpered and finally cried.

"You may hold him while I do the dishes," suggested Nancy.

"I couldn't hold a little mite like that with my hand throbbing."

"I had forgotten about that. Come and soak it again."

The baby was made comfortable, and Nancy started washing dishes. There was a large stack of baking utensils.

"Does it pay to bake like this?" asked Steve from his position beside the basin.

"David and I have had enough to live on."

"David!" shouted Steve. "Who's David?"

"The baby, Steve. Don't get so excited. He had to have a name, you know."

"And you named him David?"

"Yes. It was my own daddy's name. It's in the Bible, you know. Is there anything wrong with the name?"

"You can't call him David!"

"Why, Steve?"

"You just can't. You should have asked me first."

"You weren't here, and he had to have a name."

"You'll have to change it."

"But I can't. It's on the birth certificate."

"Well, I don't like the name, and I won't have it. Do you hear?" shouted Steve, upsetting the basin.

"I put the name David Boyd on the birth certificate. Would you rather call him Boyd?"

"Yes. Yes." Steve sat down. He looked exhausted. "Anything but David."

"Let's go to bed."

"I'll help you mop the water if you bind my hand again. It feels so much better."

# CHAPTER 17

The doors and windows were open, but little breeze penetrated the kitchen, warm from a morning of baking. The street door below opened and closed.

"Wonder who's coming." A heavy *thud, thump* was heard on the stairs.

"Come on in, Mr. Garrett," greeted Nancy.

"Here, sit and have a bite of pie and some

coffee." Steve rose and pushed his chair under the lame man.

"I don't aim to stay long. I jest wanted to know if you wanted carpenter work ag'in." Jim Garrett took a bite of blueberry pie.

"What did you have in mind, Jim?"

"My boy Tom went an' signed up for the Hudson car agency. We won't get any till the thirty-eights come out 'bout New Year, but we want to have a nice showroom ready."

"That sounds great." Steve whistled.

"Maybe we could measure off at the east side, and you could give us an idea how much 'twould cost."

Steve looked at Nancy.

"It's all right with me." Nancy tried to keep the eagerness out of her voice. She had prayed for a job for Steve these four weeks that he had been home.

"Let's go have a look," said Steve eagerly. The two men started down the stairs. "I'll be back to help deliver the pies," called Steve from the bottom step.

Promptly at five-thirty Steve came home.

"What's that?" inquired Nancy indicating the cagelike affair in Steve's hand.

"That is a pie carrier." He opened the doors and started sliding pies into it. Each pie had its own compartment so it wouldn't slide around, and the carrier held eight pies. It fit exactly in the wagon.

When Steve came home after the third trip,

Nancy laughed.

"I hope you won't mind waiting a bit on your supper. I wasn't counting on getting the pies delivered so quickly."

"I thought it would be a nice surprise." Steve went into the living room. Nancy could hear the comfortable creak of the rocker and Steve's voice quietly talking to the baby.

\*　　\*　　\*

"It's hard to believe Boyd's seven months old already," said Steve. It was Saturday evening. He was bouncing Boyd on his knee. Nancy sat on the sofa stitching away.

"There that's finished." She held up a boy's cap.

"I was wondering what it was you were working on. That looks like a pair of pants I once had."

"They weren't fit to wear anymore, and he needed a cap. It's usually even cooler than this in October."

"And you made Boyd a man's cap out of them. Your ma sure is smart, young fella. Now let's try it out."

Steve carried the baby as they strolled into the cool, peaceful evening.

"I want to show you the new showroom I'm building for the Garretts."

The yellow of new lumber shone in the setting sun. "See there," said Steve proudly.

"It looks nice, Steve."

"See that old Plymouth alongside the

101

building?"

"Um-m-m," murmured Nancy.

"Jim says I can have it for twenty bucks."

"Is that all?"

"It needs a new piston, and the brakes need fixing."

"It would be nice to have a car to deliver pies. I keep getting more orders all the time."

*     *     *

Evenings were getting shorter.

"Now, Boyd, let's see. Potatoes in the oven, onion sauce all ready, and I'll put this leftover meat in the oven." Then she hurried to the bedroom and brought Boyd's cap and coat.

"You see," she spoke as though he were a grown-up, "this is a celebration. You and I are going to help Daddy bring our car home. We won't mind if we get supper a little later tonight."

The clock on the shelf said four-thirty as she closed the door behind her and hurried down the street. "Daddy said he has about an hour's work on the cafter he quits work, but I want to use this first." She held the dust brush in her hand. "The seats need it."

Nancy snickered as they crossed the street to the side of the building where Steve was working. He seemed to be stuck in the motor head-first.

"How are you coming?"

He jumped, bumping his head. "Scare a man outa his shoes, will ya!" he laughed.

"We came to help. But I don't know if we want to ride home with such a dirty-faced man. Do we, Boyd?"

Steve joined her in a good laugh. "I guess we can remedy that."

Steve worked in silence while Nancy brushed the seats. She sat and admired the beautiful sunset. Then she heard the hood slam down. Steve was striding around the front of the car. *Blam!* went the other side of the hood.

"Here, Boyd, you stand on the floor between the back and front seat while I help Daddy pour in some gas."

"Now that we got some gas into her, let's get the motor started. See here, Nancy, put your foot on the throttle." He indicated the pedal on the floor.

"I don't know much about it."

"Just do as I tell you. Pull the choke out all the way." Steve went to the front of the car and grasped the hand crank. "Ready?"

"I guess so."

He turned the crank. "Now push the choke in halfway," he called as he started to crank again.

"That kicks like a mule. I'd better change the timing. Turn off the switch."

Nancy sat waiting as darkness gathered. Steve tinkered with the motor.

"Now!" He again took his position at the crank.

He turned and turned the crank. He rested a while and changed to the other hand. Metal clanked as the beam of the flashlight searched around under the hood.

Boyd started to cry. "Here," she reached into her apron pocket, "eat this cracker."

"Let's try again," called Steve from the front of the car.

"All right."

Steve turned the crank. The motor roared. Steve shouted. Boyd screamed. Then all was quiet.

"You killed the motor. I told you to push in the choke."

"I couldn't hear what you were saying." Nancy squirmed around and hoisted Boyd into the front seat. "Hush, baby, we have to yell to be heard. Here's another cracker."

The baby sat tight against Nancy sobbing.

Nancy almost held her breath as Steve cranked and cranked. She could hardly believe her ears when she heard the motor running above Boyd's screams.

"Slide over, Mom, and hush that baby up! We're going home."

"You're sitting on my skirt, Steve. I can't move over."

Steve pulled the Plymouth out into the street. "This is riding in style."

"Why is it smoking?" asked Nancy. A shower of water on the windshield made Steve stop suddenly.

"The radiator's leaking." Steve had to shout because Boyd was crying loudly again. He cleared the windshield and drove another block.

"I'll have to find some water to put in it," said Steve.

"Don't cry, baby," soothed Nancy. "There's just too much excitement for you, and you don't understand what's going on."

She watched Steve pour one container of water into the radiator and then another. He threw the containers into the back of the car. Nancy noticed that he was barefooted.

"Where is everyone tonight? No one's home, so I helped myself to water from Hopkins' pump."

"And you carried it in your boots?"

"What would you have done?" Tempers were getting short.

At last Steve guided the Plymouth into the alley and pulled up in front of the woodshed. He took the now-sleeping baby from Nancy and strode through the backyard. Inside the door Steve stopped and sniffed. "What we all need is something hot to eat."

# CHAPTER 18

Nancy was putting pies in the pie carriers.
"Only two carriers full. Business is slower. I'll have to hurry. Steve will soon be here." Lately it

had annoyed Steve if the pies weren't ready to carry out when he came home at five.

"Boyd," said Nancy sharply, "take your tractor into the living room. Mamma will fall over it here on the kitchen floor."

Steve had made a wooden replica of a tractor complete with a wooden man and given it to Boyd as a gift for his second birthday several weeks ago. The beloved tractor was never very far from the boy.

"Come, tractor. Come, tractor," said the boy as he started pulling it across the kitchen into the living room.

Suddenly the soft evening air was shattered by a terrible crash.

"Car hit!" screeched Boyd from his stance on the sofa.

Nancy hurried to look out the window.

"Oh! It's Daddy."

She grabbed the boy and tucked him under her arm like a sack of grain as she ran downstairs.

"I want my tractor."

"Never mind that now."

A crowd was gathering. Hot water from the broken radiator had sprayed the street, leaving a puddle.

"Steve," cried Nancy. "Are you hurt?"

"Dumb guy drove right in front of me," he mumbled. Ellis Ruhl came running out of his house without a shirt or shoes and holding up his trousers.

"Whadda ya think you're doin', Steve. You

drunkard! You ruined my new Hudson!"

Steve raised his fists toward Ellis, and then he staggered and sprawled in the puddle.

"My new Hudson ruined!" screamed Ellis. The neighborhood dogs howled. The sheriff drove up to the scene.

"He hit my car."

"I couldn't help he drove in front of me."

"He-he-I-I—" Ellis was so angry he could only swear and stutter.

Nancy helped Steve to stand up. Her heart sank when she smelled the liquor on his breath.

"He drove right in front of me."

"That's a lie. You're drunk." Ellis yelled at Steve, then turned to the sheriff. "Throw 'im in jail once. He's a hazard. Don't even know how to drive."

"You're not such a hot driver," yelled Steve. "Runnin' right in front of me."

"How about that, Ellis?" A smile played about the sheriff's mouth.

"I wasn't even in the car," sputtered the angry man. "Ask my wife. I was in the bathtub. Ask Mirandy. She'll tell you I wasn't in the car. How could I have pulled in front of 'im?"

"Calm down, Ellis. I believe you. You've got your trousers on backward. That's proof enough that you put them on in a hurry, but what was the excuse when you parked your car?"

"What do you mean? I parked in front of my house. It's this drunkard who don't know how to drive."

"How is it," asked the sheriff, "that you parked on the wrong side of the street?"

The men standing about guffawed.

"Get off the street both of you before I fine you both." The sheriff got into his car and drove away.

Steve started to get into his car and fell down in the mud again. Nancy was so humiliated that she couldn't think properly.

"Go into the house and get cleaned up for supper," she commanded. To her surprise he obeyed. With determined steps she climbed into the car and placed Boyd on the front seat beside her. She started the engine and drove it across the street, around the corner, and into the alley beside the woodshed.

Upstairs Steve sat at the table as though in a daze. Nancy slammed the kettle lid after she had dished a plate of soup. It thudded on the table as she set it before him.

"There ain't no need fer you to get so angry," growled Steve. "I can't help he drove in front of me."

"Eat!" commanded Nancy through set teeth. "I guess someone else poured the liquor down your throat too. You look like a pig."

"Piggy. Oink! Oink!" crowed Boyd.

"Be still and eat your supper," ordered his mother. Boyd's eyes widened. Something was wrong. Mamma had taught him to say oink like a pig.

"Take care of Boyd. I'm going to deliver the

pies." Nancy put on her sweater and tied a scarf about her head. She took the pie carrier and started toward the kitchen door. Before she realized what was happening, Steve was by her side.

"Here, that's too heavy for you." He took the pie carrier from her with a jerk. The kitchen door swung back against the wall under his unsteady hand and shook the house.

"Steve!" Nancy's shout was drowned out by the *bump, bump, bump* on the stairs. Shocked, she stood rooted to the kitchen floor and counted thirteen bumps and a final crash against the door at the bottom of the stairs. Boyd screamed and cried.

Mrs. Randall opened the door and peered into the hall, mop in hand. "Are you hurt, Steve?"

Nancy held firm to the handrail as she tried to pick her way down to the foot of the stairs trying her best to avoid stepping into lemon, cherry, or blueberry filling. Steve was plastered from head to foot with pie fillings of all flavors. It was obvious that his right arm was broken.

"This is the first time," Mrs. Randall clipped her words short, "that my walls have been decorated with pie fillings. You folks will clean them, paint them, and get out of our apartment. We are considering having evening dental appointments. We can't have such nonsense going on." The door closed behind her.

Nancy sat down in the pie-filling mess and cried, "Where will I start?"

# CHAPTER 19

Nancy thought she had never been so tired. Tears fell into her scrub pail. Boyd stood at the top of the stairs.

"Mama, I'm hungry." It was past lunchtime.

"Get some crackers."

"Don't want crackers," he pouted as a knock sounded on the door behind Nancy.

"Hello." Sally's dark head appeared around the door. "You poor girl. Are you still scrubbing?"

"If I could only have gotten to cleaning this pie-filling mess up before it dried," wailed Nancy.

"You should have told me. I would have come and helped."

"I don't want to go begging for help."

"That's what family and friends are for."

More tears fell into Nancy's scrub pail. Without comment Sally edged her way around her sister-in-law. In a short while Boyd was fed and napping.

"Come on up and have some lunch."

"I'm not hungry," said Nancy as she washed her hands at the kitchen faucet.

"I'm hungry, and you may as well keep me company."

"These tomatoes and the lettuce from your garden taste so good. I suppose I was hungrier than I thought. I haven't been able to think of

110

anything except the scrubbing and taking care of Steve. Boyd's been so grouchy."

"He's probably reflecting the mood of his parents."

"Anyone would be upset under the circumstances."

"I didn't mean to imply you don't have a reason. I was only trying to console you by saying he probably isn't sick. How is Steve?"

"The infection in the broken bone is all gone. His fever is gone also."

"He hasn't been to church. . . ."

"He says he doesn't want folks gawking at him with his arm all tied up. It hurts and he can't sit that long. He sits at the bar longer than any church service lasts," said Nancy bitterly.

Sally tied a scarf over her head and the two girls started scrubbing with a will.

"Looks like we are done," sighed Nancy. "Now to paint it and hunt a house to live in."

"I'll help you paint and hunt a house if I can."

"Why are you so good to me, Sally?"

"Christ did so much for all of us. I love you. You're my sister."

\* \* \*

The new green paint glistened in the afternoon sun as Nancy went slowly down the stairs waiting for Boyd to step down one step at a time.

"We're going house hunting in style today, sweetheart."

111

"My tractor."

"You won't need that. Grandma Yoder has toys. You are going to stay with her while Aunt Sally and I go to buy a house."

Nancy felt in her purse for her brand-new driver's license.

Jim Garrett had put in a secondhand radiator and taken out the dents. Nancy had painted the car herself.

"I'm glad Mrs. Randall allowed us another month to find a place to live. She was so pleased with the paint job."

She stopped in front of the open woodshed door.

"It's gone, Boyd. Our car's gone! Daddy must have taken it at noon."

"We'll have to take the wagon. Oh!"

Nancy sank to the ground beside the wagon. Obviously Steve had backed the car out without moving the wagon far enough. The wooden bed was splintered and the wheels bent beyond repair.

Boyd sat silently beside his weeping mother until he went to sleep. She didn't even look up when footsteps approached her.

"Nancy!" exclaimed Sally. "You're two hours late. Your mother is frantic with worry. What happened?"

"The car. The wagon," sobbed Nancy. "Every way I turn is wrong."

"I'll take Boyd to Mother Yoder. You get cleaned up till I come back, and we'll see if Axel

Smith is still in the mood for selling the little house up the street."

It was Bill who came for Nancy. He drove fast across the country road. Dust rose in swirls behind them the five miles into the country to the Axel residence.

"My mister's out in the barn milking the cows," Mrs. Smith told them.

"Well," drawled Smith leaning his head against the cow he was milking, "I figgered you wasn't interested in the place anymore."

"Car problems came up," was Bill's comment.

"You got the hundred dollars down?"

"I could only scrape up fifty," declared Nancy, "but I need a place to live so badly, and there are no places to rent."

"I'll loan you fifty more," put in Bill, "but I don't have it with me. I'll bring it out after the store closes tonight. I don't like to leave my wife tending the store longer than I have to."

"Soon's I get finished milkin' old Sapphiry here, we can go to the county seat and fix it up."

Steve was asleep on the sofa when Nancy returned to the house at seven-thirty.

"Steve!"

"Eh. . . ."

"Wake up!"

He sat up unsteadily. "What you wake me up in the middle of the night fer?"

"It's not the middle of the night. It's only seven-thirty. I bought the Axel Smith house this afternoon."

"Are you crazy? That's four blocks away."

"Four blocks away from what? Iky's?"

"It's a beat-up old house."

"I'm giving only five hundred dollars for it. Last week when we looked at it, you thought it was all right. Yesterday you wanted to buy it. Tomorrow when you're sober, I think you'll want it too."

# CHAPTER 20

"You won't need to worry about me going into harvest this year," said Steve as they sat down to their noon meal.

"Are the grasshoppers that bad?"

"There just won't be any wheat crop."

"A body don't see those things as well when you ride in a car as when you walk."

"Elmer Burns' crop is all eaten," said Steve. "Even Ma Pletcher's begonias are eaten."

Boyd climbed down from his stool and left while his parents sat about the table and talked.

"Stay out of the bake shop," called Nancy.

"I will, Mamma." He spoke like a three-year-old man. A large room across the front of the house had been made into a bake shop. One small room behind it was their kitchen, the other a living room. The stairs with a tiny bathroom under it was between the two back rooms. There were two bedrooms above. The promise Steve had made a year ago to pipe running water into the kitchen and bakery was still unfulfilled.

"Boyd," Steve called. "I hear water running. What are you doing?"

"I'm washing my hands."

"Get 'em washed and don't waste water. Water costs money."

"What about the grasshoppers?" asked Nancy.

"As I was saying, the government has declared it a disaster. There's a station at Fullers' old creamery building where they give out this poison. It has to be mixed fresh every day. Someone has to spread it. I've made a spreader out of an old oil drum and differential from a car. Jim Garrett says it's a good idea. You tow the spreader along behind your truck, fill the drum, and it spreads the poison."

"Will it work?"

"Sure it'll work, but I'll need two more dollars to finish this first one. I have eight. It needs a little welding. When I sell or rent this one, I'll have money to make another. That's right! I left the roll top unlocked and my plans lying on top when you called me for dinner." Steve rushed through the bake shop to the living room.

"Boyd! No one is to touch my desk." A loud slap, followed by a high piercing scream, sent Nancy running to the living room.

Steve reached for the yardstick he had been using to draw his plans. Screams and whacks mingled.

"Steve! Stop!" cried Nancy.

Steve was possessed with a wild anger.

"He's had enough, Steve," shouted Nancy above the terrible screams. When the stick broke and Steve kept on beating, she threw herself against Steve.

"Get outa here," he roared.

"Quit! Quit!" cried Nancy. She wrenched the screaming boy from Steve's grasp and ran upstairs with him.

"What did you take out of Daddy's desk?"

"Nothing! Nothing!"

"Don't ever touch Daddy's desk again. You touched the one thing he has forbidden anyone to touch." She saw large purple welts already rising across his small back.

*If he would only stop drinking*, she thought to herself as she went downsairs, *He wouldn't be as touchy*.

Her heart was heavy as she started to stir up the butterscotch cake for Tom Garrett's little girl.

Suddenly Steve towered over her. "I guess I'll have to finish the job now." He jerked her roughly by the shoulder and beat her mercilessly.

"Now when I set to punish my son hereafter, you won't interfere. Hear me?"

Pain shot through her body. She couldn't speak.

"Do you hear?"

"You beat him too hard."

"I will beat anyone who tampers with my

116

desk. I told you that long ago."

"Did he harm your plans?"

"No."

"What did he spoil?"

"That's not the point. He disobeyed orders."

"Why do you guard the desk so carefully as though it contains some secret?"

"I said let it alone! You and all others!" Steve stamped out of the house.

# CHAPTER 21

"Mamma! You aren't even listening," said Boyd loudly.

"Sh-h-h—Daddy's asleep," warned Nancy.

"Why isn't Daddy going to church this morning?"

Nancy searched for the right words. How did one tell a five-year-old boy that his daddy had been drinking the night before and couldn't lift his head off the pillow? She couldn't lie and have Boyd lose confidence in her.

"He doesn't feel well." Nancy felt that this was true.

"What's wrong with Daddy?"

"I'm not a doctor," evaded Nancy.

"He throwed-up last night. I heard it, and I prayed he wouldn't die."

She caught her breath. She had been thankful that Boyd had a room of his own in this house. By

117

closing his door at night, she thought he wouldn't hear if Steve came home drunk.

"Daddy won't die will he, Mamma?"

Silently she prayed for an answer. She swallowed the lump in her throat.

"I hope Daddy doesn't die now, sweetheart." Before Boyd could think of another question, she added, "Please eat your oatmeal. It's time to start walking to church."

"Must we walk to church? What's wrong with the Plymouth again?"

"Daddy hit the back of the garage when he wasn't feeling well last night. Come on, put on your boots."

"I went to tell Daddy good-bye, but he couldn't hear me. Something smelled awful in the bedroom. Did you give him some medicine that smelled so bad?"

"Let's hurry, Boyd. Stop asking questions. When Daddy is sick, you shouldn't even go in his room." Boyd raised his eyes in wonder at the sharpness in his mother's voice.

Boyd loved to sing. He enjoyed going to Sunday school. Nancy never had the problem of keeping him still in church except to tell him to save his questions until after services were over.

\*    \*    \*

"Why are you girls walking home with me?" Boyd asked his cousins as they trudged along the snow-slushed road.

"Papa said your mamma gets a lot of exercise. It's more 'propriate for younger legs to walk. You're comin' to our house for dinner anyway," answered Ruth, the talkative twin.

"Our family's too big," chimed in Becky, "or we'd always take you to church. Papa said two-and-a-half miles is too far to walk to church."

Rhoda was a serious girl and seemed older than ten years. "Don't talk so much," she admonished her sisters.

The happy foursome started singing. They sang several songs as they walked along.

"What's a drunkard?" asked Boyd.

"Somebody that drinks something he shouldn't," Ruth informed him importantly.

"Like what?"

"Well, strong stuff."

"Soda pop?"

"Stronger'n that, silly."

"Why do you ask such questions anyway, Boyd?" asked Rhoda.

"Well we just sang 'no drunkard can enter that beautiful home' an' I wanted to make sure I wasn't one," said Boyd seriously. "I want to go to heaven."

"You have to buy it at Iky's."

"Iky's!" screeched Boyd in surprise. "Don't Iky sell good stuff?"

"Don't you ever buy his stuff," warned Ruth.

"I don't even have money."

"I mean when you get big enough to get money."

119

"Why?"

"It's a wicked place," snapped Rhoda. "Quit talking about it."

Boyd's boots went sloshing in the soft, muddy snow in the middle of the road. Rhoda daintily picked her way while Ruth's and Becky's feet crunched on the fresh, clean snow beside the road.

"I'm gonna pray real hard," said Boyd, stopping to catch his breath, "that my dad will get better. He missed four Sunday schools a'ready. he must feel awful to miss so many. I would."

"Me too," said Becky.

"Oh yes!" exclaimed Ruth.

"And I," was Rhoda's rejoinder. "If two or three pray for the same thing, God will give it. So let's all pray for Uncle Steve to get better."

"He gets sick on Saturday night, so we have to pray special hard on Saturday nights," said Boyd.

\* \* \*

The sunset was turning to purple and orange as Nancy and Boyd started to walk home that winter evening.

"I'll take you home, Sis," Bill said.

"I feel like I'd like to walk and enjoy the sunset."

They walked along in silence with only the crunching of their boots in the snow.

"I like to walk in the snow. Don't you, Mamma?"

"Yes."

"Can we fix the Plymouth till next Sunday?"

"Jim Garrett said the last time that six times hitting the same old fenders was too much."

"Then we will have to walk to church again."

"You just told me you like to walk."

They had reached the pavement now and turned the corner onto Main Street. Iky's bar on the other side of the street was already brightly lighted.

"Let's cross the street," Boyd tugged on his mother's hand.

"No, wait until we are by Iky's place before we cross."

"Is Iky's bad?"

"He. . . ." Nancy hesitated. Boyd's questions were so hard to answer. "His place isn't nice."

"Does he sell bad stuff?"

"He sells strong drink, Boyd. When you drink it, you don't know what you're doing, and a person who drinks it—. . . ."

"Is a drunkard and can't go to heaven," finished Boyd.

"Why are you asking all this?"

"We sang it in Sunday school this morning, and I asked the girls on the way home about it. Ruth said it's wicked to buy at Iky's and I shouldn't buy there when I get big 'nough to have money."

"Don't ever go there," warned Nancy.

"Then how come Daddy goes there?"

Nancy was horrified. "What makes you think

he does?"

"He went in there last week when we delivered pies."

"And took you in!" gasped Nancy.

"No. He said, 'wait here a minute.'"

"Maybe he wanted to sell some pies to Iky," said Nancy weakly.

"Oh, does he sell pies too?"

"I don't know. Let's talk about something else."

# CHAPTER 22

Nancy took a final swipe of the dishrag around the dishpan and hung it on its nail.

"I'd better get a hammer and fix that broken board at the top of the stairs before someone falls on it." Steve stretched to the shelf behind the kitchen stove and brought his toolbox down.

"On a Saturday night?" asked Nancy.

"It's only six-thirty."

"How come Boyd went to bed so early?" asked Steve. "He could have helped me."

"He has been going to bed promptly at six o'clock every Saturday night for the past couple of weeks."

Steve went to the garage and selected a board. When he returned, he asked, "Do you care if I saw the board in your clean kitchen? It's cold outside."

"Sawdust isn't hard to sweep up. You needn't

saw it out in the cold."

"Ah-h-h," said Steve sinking into a chair, "if I don't need to go out anymore, I think I'll take off my boots."

He padded across the kitchen. "I'll have to go up and measure how much to saw off."

He was almost at the top of the stairs when he heard a voice. *Now who could Boyd have up here? We thought he was going to bed early and here he is entertaining company in his room. I'll have to look into this.*

He walked softly toward Boyd's door and was about to enter; then he stopped.

A slit of sunset showed around the slightly opened door. It looked like a heap of blankets piled beside the bed. Steve shivered in the cold. Little heat came up the stairs. The pile of blankets moved, revealing Boyd's head leaning on the side of the bed.

"Ruth and Rhoda and Becky are praying hard for Daddy too, God." Steve heard the voice muffled by blankets. "Don't let him get sick again on Saturday night. He wants to feel good to go to Sunday school. Thanks for 'lowing him to be well 'nough to go for three weeks now, but Rhoda says we must keep praying."

Steve backed away. He stole down the stairs into the darkened bakeshop. He leaned against the counter, drawing out his large, red hanky. Finally he went into the bathroom, blew his nose, and washed his face before going to the kitchen to saw his board.

The bakeshop smelled spicy. Steve sniffed. "My nose tells me you're baking peppernut cookies."

"What a sharp nose you have," laughed Nancy, "but it's pumpkin pies tonight."

"Do they have to be delivered?"

"They're too warm, but I had to bake some of them tonight to get a head start on tomorrow's baking."

Steve put his toolbox on the kitchen shelf and washed his hands at the sink he'd installed in the bakery. "Sure is nice to have hot running water in here," he commented. "It didn't take long either when I set my mind to it."

"About two weeks of staying home evenings," Nancy told him.

"I know," he sighed. He stood staring into the December night.

"Do you have any baking for the day after tomorrow?"

"Just for our own Christmas dinner."

"Where's Boyd?"

"He's delivering cookies."

Steve edged close to his wife. "Tell you what. If you could manage, I'd like to surprise Boyd and take him to Mason City shopping the day before Christmas. If I help you with the baking tomorrow, could you bake our pies too and go along?"

"Oh, Steve." Nancy was too surprised to say

more.

"We couldn't buy much," he added quickly, "but the trip would be something different for both of you. Boyd will be in school next year, you know."

"We'd have so much fun," breathed Nancy. "Let's not tell. Sh! Here he comes."

* * *

A loud jangle brought both Steve and Nancy to a sitting position in bed. They shivered in the cold darkness.

"Wh-wh-at was that?" grumbled Steve sleepily.

"The alarm," laughed Nancy. "Silly, don't you remember? It's the day before Christmas."

Steve's feet hit the floor at the same time he turned on the light. It was too cold to dawdle.

"It's four-twenty," said Steve as he started toward Boyd's bedroom. "You go ahead and get breakfast. I'll get Boyd. We want to make that five-o'clock bus to Mason City."

Nancy had the oatmeal cooking and the coffee started when Steve carried Boyd into the kitchen where Nancy had his clean clothes laid out on a chair next to the stove.

Boyd tottered and would have fallen if Steve had not caught him. "Wake up, Boyd! Let's get dressed." Steve helped him into his clothes.

"It's dark," whimpered Boyd.

"Eat," ordered his mother.

Steve was as excited as a small boy. He went to the living room and brought Boyd's outer wraps.

"Are we going to church in the dark?" asked Boyd as his dad stuffed his hands into the mittens.

"It's not a church day. Here, I'll carry you. Lock the door, Mama. There comes the bus."

"We're going away on the bus!" Boyd was wide awake now.

*   *   *

"Mason City's next," Steve told Boyd. "There are a lot of big stores. I'll buy you one thing for your Christmas present. Something that doesn't cost too much."

Boyd's eyes were wide with wonder as the bus stopped in the center of town and they alighted. The stores were brightly lighted and decorated for the Christmas holidays. Dampness penetrated their heavy coats out on the streets, but Steve, Nancy, and Boyd didn't notice it.

Boyd looked small and scared when Steve lifted him to a high stool between himself and his mother at the dime-store lunch counter.

"Let's have oyster stew, Nan. Would you like that?"

"Yes." Nancy looked up at her husband lovingly. *Life is so wonderful,* she thought. *It must go on like this.*

"Like the stew, Boyd?"

"Um-huh," beamed the little man on the stool

between his parents.

"Now if Mamma is finished," stated Steve as he helped Boyd spoon the last of the stew into his mouth, "we'll go buy a present for her first."

Steve led the way toward Walmer's Department Store. Boyd clutched his daddy about the neck when he held him as they rode on the elevator.

"Hold tight to Daddy. We're going to buy Mamma a sweater."

"Not a store-bought sweater!"

"Sure. Why not?"

"I never had one. I don't even know what size to buy."

Nancy's face was rosy from the excitement and cold as she tried on the green sweater that Steve declared was made for her.

"The green reminds me of green wheat, and your hair is like ripened wheat," said Steve softly when the clerk went to wrap the sweater. "The ripened wheat is showing signs of gray in it," he added sadly.

"We'll go to the toy department next." Up one more floor on the elevator. Boyd wasn't frightened as much now.

His eyes and head could hardly turn fast enough to take it all in.

"Would you like a teddy bear, Son?" asked Steve looking at a woolly one.

"I'd like this book, Daddy."

"A book!" exploded Steve.

Boyd nodded his head affirmatively. He

pointed to a book about a little boy and his dog. Nancy leafed through it.

"Are you sure?" asked Nancy.

"Yes."

Steve bought the book and a toy truck. The clock on the bank building said three o'clock.

"We'd better get to the bus stop by four o'clock." Steve told Nancy. Snowflakes had begun to flutter.

"We didn't buy anything for Daddy," said Boyd.

"We'll have to go in this dime store and buy warm socks for Daddy."

The store was crowded so that they couldn't walk very fast. Steve and Nancy saw the curtained booth at the same time. A sign declared that one could have a picture taken and wait fifteen minutes while it was developed.

"Let's get Boyd's picture taken," said Steve excitedly.

"Do we have time?"

They shopped for the socks while they were waiting for the picture to be developed.

"You've got a fine son," said the man as he exchanged the photograph for Steve's dime.

"That sure is cute," declared Steve.

"He looks like you did when you were that size."

"How do you know how I looked?" demanded Steve roughly.

"Why, that picture you had in your wallet. Let's get it out and compare."

128

"No. It's gone. Forget it," said Steve crossly. "Let's get to the bus station."

# CHAPTER 23

The large oven was filled with pies. "I do appreciate this oven, Steve."

"The bakery business has been good these past two years."

The door opened with a jingle of bells, and Steve went to the front to wait on the customer. Four o'clock in the afternoon was a busy time for the Buttercup Bakery. Persons on the way home from work stopped in for baked goods.

Henry Cameron, a neighbor of the Yoders, stopped in every Friday evening. "Anything left over from other days to take to Bill's?" he asked.

"Only a sack of cookies this evening," said Nancy.

"Bill's seven children can stow away a lot of cookies," laughed Henry.

Nancy heard the back door open and close. *Boyd is late getting home from school*, she thought as she went on chatting with Henry

"It's past five," said Steve as he lowered the front door shade and turned out the lights.

Nancy was in the kitchen taking supper from the oven. "Roast chicken, Boyd's favorite meat." She straightened her back. "Where is that boy? I heard him come in the back door while Henry

Cameron was in the shop talking. That was an hour ago."

"He's probably upstairs reading," said Steve.

Nancy went to the foot of the stairs. "Boyd, come to supper."

No answer.

Nancy called again. "Boyd, supper will get cold."

"I don't want supper," came a small voice from above.

"Well," Nancy was up the stairs before she finished the sentence. "He must be sick if he doesn't want to eat. What's wrong, Son?"

"Boyd! What happened?" she cried. She was horrified at the disfigured little face that showed above the covers. It would have been almost unrecognizable anywhere else. His pillow was spotted with blood.

Boyd pulled the covers farther up and turned away. His sniffling was all that broke the silence in the room.

"What happened, Boyd? We'll have to get your face cleaned up."

He would not answer.

"What's taking so long?" shouted Steve angrily. He had been ill-tempered lately. She hurried to the top of the stairs.

"Let's leave him sleep."

Steve was already coming up the stairs. He strode into the room. "What's the matter with him?"

"What in the. . .? What happened?"

"N-n-ot-th-ing," sobbed the heap under the covers.

Steve grabbed the covers off the boy. "It don't look like nothing. Get up and speak out!" Roughly he stood him beside the bed. Boyd winced with pain.

"What tore your shirt? Your pants—new ones—are muddy and torn. Now tell me what happened before I lick you good." Steve reached for his belt.

"He's beat up enough," pleaded Nancy.

"He can talk and say what happened." He turned to Boyd. "I said speak!"

"We—we—" he sobbed, "was a fight."

"That I can see. What happened is what I want to know."

"It was just [sob—sniffle] a argument."

"What about?"

"Just nothin'."

"You oughta have something to fight about first. Who were you fighting with?"

Boyd started crying afresh.

"Can't we let it alone?" begged Nancy.

"No. I want to know who he fought with and what for." He grabbed Boyd roughly.

Boyd screamed.

"Stop yer hollering, and tell me who you fought."

Boyd cried harder.

Steve sat on the bed and turned Boyd over his knees. Nancy's screams mingled with Boyd's as Steve struck.

"Steve, he's cut below the tear in his pants. Please quit."

"Chuck Wilson, Chuck Wilson!" yelled Boyd as loud as he could.

He set the boy on his feet. "Now why do you have to be so stubborn? You could have told me without getting licked. I'm going to eat, and both of you better get down to the table if you know what's good for you."

Nancy followed Boyd down the stairs. His little feet went stomp, stomp, stomp; he could scarcely walk.

Steve had already cut the chicken.

"Dish up," he ordered Nancy.

"Sit down, Boyd."

Boyd edged himself stiffly onto the chair. Nancy reached to help him.

"Sit down to the table once," roared Steve. "If he wants to get himself into a fight, you don't need to pamper him."

Without the blessing, Steve started eating. Boyd slowly put small bites into his mouth. Nancy almost choked on her food as she saw the pained expression that accompanied each tiny bite.

Steve shoved back his chair.

"I'm going to see these Wilsons and find out what happened."

"Oh, Steve, no!"

"If I can't find out from my own boy, I'll find out some other way. No one is gonna pick on my boy and get away with it. And if Boyd picked the fight, he's gonna get a lickin' he won't forget so quick." He looked ominously at Boyd. "You'll do more than just edge onto that chair if you picked the fight. You'll have to stand to eat." The door slammed behind his angry figure.

Boyd began to cry wildly.

"He—he'll—be more mad—when—he knows—"

"Knows what, Boyd?" pleaded his mother.

He cried and cried. "Can't I go to Grand-ma's?"

"Can't you tell Mamma what's the matter?"

"I—I—slapped him first. That—that's pick-in'—the—fight, ain't it?"

"Why did you slap the boy, Boyd?" asked Nancy sternly.

"He—he said—something." Sobs choked him.

"What did he say?"

Nancy took him to the bathroom and started to bathe him. Boyd retched. Nancy's heart was wrenched when she unclothed him and saw the scars of a terrible battle. The scratches beneath his trousers were deep and edged in purple. She wondered if his nose was broken.

"Chuck hit me with a board."

"How big is this Chuck?"

"He's in seventh grade."

"Oh, Boyd, whatever made you hit a big boy like that? You aren't taught in the Bible or in Sunday school to fight like this. What would your teacher say?"

"Wouldn't—she—she hit someone if they said, 'Your daddy is the worst drunkard that lives in Dry Forks'?"

Nancy caught herself at the washbowl. She felt faint. "Did Chuck say that?"

"That's a bad word to call my daddy, isn't it?" sobbed Boyd.

"You should have just let it pass, Boyd. It doesn't matter what people say." She tried to choose the right words. "If it isn't true, what does it matter what they say? And if it is true, fighting won't change it."

"It isn't true. It isn't true, Mamma. I'll hit him again if he says it again."

"I said," Nancy took him by his arm and looked intently at the bruised face, "you are not to hit Chuck Wilson again or anyone else. Do you hear? I'll try to keep Daddy from whipping you this time because perhaps you didn't know better. The Bible says if anyone hits us, we are to turn the other cheek; but never does it say to hit someone, and you are not to do so. Do you understand?"

"Yes, Mamma." Clad in clean, warm pajamas, Boyd climbed stiffly up the stairs.

# CHAPTER 24

"Mamma," Boyd stood beside the counter on which his mother was working.

"Yes?"

"I've got a job."

"You what?" Nancy put the cake decorator down and looked at him.

"I've got a job."

"You're only twelve years old. . . ."

"But I scrub your floors, and Mrs. Compton said if my scrubbing is good enough for you, she is willing to try it."

"What about your schoolwork?"

"I will be working only on Saturday until school's out. That's only four weeks."

"And after school is out?" questioned his mother.

"I'll work every morning cleaning up the cabins that were rented during the night to tourists. During harvest I'll need to work harder. I'll get forty cents for every floor I scrub. I can still deliver the baked things in the afternoon or evening when Dad—when he doesn't feel like it."

"Why all the concern about earning money?"

"Rhoda's going to high school, and I'm going too."

"But you're only in seventh grade."

"It'll take a long time to save enough money to buy books for high school."

"We'll see how it works out," said Nancy. She watched the thin figure disappear into the kitchen.

"I'll make supper, Mamma," he called, "if you tell me what to make."

135

"There's baked beans in the oven. You may wash the lettuce and set the table. I won't be through in the shop for a while."

She kept on working. After Boyd had finished the work in the kitchen, he brought his books into the bakery and worked on his lessons. He waited on the customers. Finally, when it was five o'clock, he locked the door and lowered the shade.

"The days are getting longer," Nancy remarked at last. "It's six-thirty and still daylight."

The clock in the kitchen struck seven.

"We may as well eat, Mamma," said Boyd quietly. "He's not coming home for supper."

She felt heartsick. She wasn't hungry. Boyd hadn't been fooled, but knew she was only pretending to be busy in order to wait a little longer for Steve.

"Daddy hasn't come home for supper once this week."

The ticking of the clock sounded loud in the quiet kitchen. Silverware scraped on the two plates.

"Why does Daddy do it?" cried Boyd at last.

"I don't know." Nancy took her hanky from her apron pocket and blew her nose. She must not cry in front of Boyd. He had seen too many tears. Noisily she started clearing the table.

"It seems like Daddy is two different people," said Boyd heavily. "He's so good and kind for a long time, and then all of a sudden he's—he's— different."

"Boyd, promise me you will never touch a drop of liquor."

"I never will, Mamma. I wouldn't want to drink something that turned me from a kind and good daddy into a—a—" Tears crept down his lean face.

"I'm glad you have become a Christian, but the devil is tricky. You can never let down any bars."

"What do you mean—let down any bars?"

"The devil can get you into sin even if you are a Christian if you don't watch and pray. I know—he did me." She hadn't meant to say so much.

"I don't understand," said the perplexed boy.

"You're too young to understand."

"Understand what?"

"That you shouldn't—shouldn't date non-Christians."

"I would never do that, Mamma. That would be foolish. Where would I go with a non-Christian girl? What could I talk about to her? She wouldn't want to talk about the Bible. That's what Brother Burns preaches."

Nancy lowered her head. Her young son understood what she had refused to accept when eighteen years old.

"But I didn't listen," sobbed his mother.

"Listen to what, Mamma? You never dated non-Christians, did you?"

She nodded her head affirmatively. "Daddy wasn't a Christian when I met him, and I wouldn't listen—not to the preacher, my mother, or anyone. I acted foolishly, and I have reaped only tears for what I have sown. I've had a bountiful harvest."

"Oh, Mamma!"

They cried silently together.

\* \* \*

Nancy peeked into the kitchen. Her sigh hung heavy in the quiet summer evening air of the bakeshop. She had heard Steve come in the back door an hour ago.

*Just as I thought. He just sits there.*

Boyd's singing stopped when he came in and saw Steve in the kitchen.

"Hello, Dad," said Boyd quietly. "Did you get a job today?"

"No one's building stuff right now, and if they are," he added bitterly, "they hire a big outfit to do it."

There was an awkward silence. Finally Steve spoke. "Can't you loan me a couple dollars, Son?"

"What for?"

"Food."

"Mamma bought groceries yesterday."

"Now don't get smart. When I was a boy, I gave all my money to my dad."

"Did he use it to buy liquor?"

Angrily Steve stood and slapped Boyd's mouth.

"Don't sass back to me. You claim to be a

Christian, yet you sass your dad."

"I don't claim to be a Christian. My life should show it."

"Shut up," growled Steve. "I fed and clothed you when you were little; now you won't even loan me a nickel."

"I have loaned you a lot of money since I started working over two years ago, Dad. You've never paid any—"

"See! You keep track of every penny you give me."

"Dad, I'd give you every penny I earned if I were sure you wouldn't buy liquor. Besides, school starts in two weeks, and I don't have any books."

"If you'd listen to me, you wouldn't need any books. Get out and work like I had to when I was yer age," shouted Steve.

"I'm going to high school, Dad, if I have to borrow every book I use. Someday I even hope to go to college."

Books weren't mentioned for almost a week. Boyd avoided speaking to Steve.

"It's too hard to know what to say, Mom," he exclaimed. "I hate to say no when he asks for money."

Just then Steve came from the living room.

Nancy was setting the kitchen to rights before going to bed.

"I'll take you to Mason City tomorrow, Son," declared Steve; "you can buy used books in a big city."

"Thanks, Dad." Boyd's face glowed. "It's a big baking day for Mom, though. Can't we wait until Monday?"

"I didn't even invite your ma to go along," said Steve evenly. "We are going tomorrow."

This was not a pleasant trip like the one Boyd remembered when they all went together. It was late when they arrived in the city.

"We have just enough time to buy the books before the stores close."

Boyd held the list of books he would need in his hand. Steve rummaged through the used books. He insisted that the oldest and most shopworn books were good enough.

"There's no sense to spend good money on books when you can get some for less," Steve insisted.

Boyd held the paper sack containing the books as they left the store. They went to a cheap rooming house.

"I'll need some of that money to get a room for the night."

"Why don't we just go on home? There's a bus as late as ten."

"Now don't get smart. I gave in and got your books; now give the money."

Boyd started to take some money from his wallet. Steve grabbed the wallet and walked into the rooming house. "Now come along and quit being so stubborn."

To the man behind the registrar's desk he said, "I want a cheap room, the cheapest you got."

At the door of the room, Steve took the key and unlocked it. It was on the fourth floor. There was no window, and it was dirty. Boyd shrank back.

"Come on before I give you a licking as big as you are. Now don't you stir from this room until I get back." The door closed behind Boyd. He felt sick when he heard the key turn in the lock. Tears welled up in his eyes.

*He didn't give my wallet back.* Boyd knew he was too big to cry, but who was to hear him? *God's here,* he told himself quietly, as he read his Testament that he carried in his pocket. Through the long hot night he prayed and at last decided he would not worry his mother by telling her that he had spent the night alone in a dirty, cheap room.

"She may as well not know that he took my money either, unless she asks about it."

# CHAPTER 25

"I guess it's my fault," Nancy said partly under her breath.

"What's your fault, Mamma?" asked Boyd.

"There isn't money for you to go to college."

"Don't say that, Mamma. You've worked so hard all these years." It was not often, now that Boyd was a man of nineteen-and-a-half, that he called her Mamma instead of Mom.

"But it was I who was careless and lost the bank deposit last week. I wouldn't feel so badly but that's the third time in the past six months that I've done the same trick. I'm getting old and forgetful."

"Old! You're only forty-five. You just have too much to worry about."

"My hair is getting too gray to deny that I'm on the way up in years."

Boyd perched on the high stool. Nancy sat beside him on another. They counted pennies, nickels, and dimes behind the drawn shades of the bakery.

"Ninety-nine dollars!" Boyd whistled softly between his teeth.

"I'm going to hide it until I can take it to the bank tomorrow." He disappeared up the stairs.

Boyd returned with a long slim envelope which he laid on the counter beside his mother.

"Marshall Bible College," read Nancy. Sudden tears rushed to her eyes. She turned and went into the kitchen. She hadn't turned quickly enough.

"I thought you wanted me to go," he said perplexedly. "Why are you sad?"

"I'll miss you, but I'm not sad because you're going. The money—"

"I have half the price already. If the Lord wants me to prepare to serve Him, He will supply the rest."

"I wish I had as much faith as you have."

"But, Mom, I learned it from you."

Nancy groaned inwardly. "Then I should never go to the door and look down the street apprehensively when it's time for Daddy to come home. I should have faith that he will come home sober at the proper time."

"His odd jobs make his time for coming home so irregular."

"We go to bed so many nights listening for faltering footsteps."

With heavy hearts they went to bed again that night without Steve. They prayed and resolved they would not listen for faltering footsteps.

Nancy slapped twice at the bumblebee in her pillow before she realized it was Steve snoring beside her.

Softly she crept from bed. It was only five in the morning, but she had had a wonderful rest. She'd get the Thursday baking started early.

Breakfast seemed like a festival. Steve was with them for breakfast for the first time in months.

"I won't be home for lunch, Mom. If I eat lunch between serving customers right there in the filling station, I can be home by five and help to deliver the pies."

"I'll deliver pies today," said Steve. "I'm through fixing Compton's screens."

"A day of pie-baking such as this," announced Nancy at two o'clock in the afternoon, "calls for a glass of lemonade."

"I'll load the pies into the truck while you're making it," called Steve as he went out the back door to bring the truck around to the front.

"I didn't even hear you come home last night," said Nancy as they sipped lemonade.

"It wasn't late," smiled Steve. "I'm glad you got a good rest. Work goes so much better when we get a good rest."

She watched Steve drive away and then turned to the sinkful of dishes. She sang as she ran hot water to do them. The bell jangled.

"Good aft—Mother! This is a surprise. Come on in."

"I'll help."

"When you come to visit, I'm not going to be working all the time. I need to rest my feet. Let's go into the kitchen."

"It's cool in here." Mrs. Yoder fanned herself with her sunbonnet.

"I'll get you some lemonade." Nancy poured a tall glass of frosty lemonade for her mother and refilled her own.

"Steve and I just had some, but I could use another glass."

"Is Steve home?"

"He went to deliver pies." She wondered at her mother's question. She knew that her mother hadn't walked eight blocks just to visit.

"Nancy," her mother folded and unfolded the corner of her apron, "Boyd still wants to go to college?"

She nodded. "He sent in his registration yesterday."

"He has enough money then?"

"He has faith that he will get it somehow."

"I've got it."

"Oh, no, Mother. You can't loan—"

"It's not that. It's your money."

"My money!"

"When your baby girl died, the neighbors made up a purse of money to help you. You refused it. Elmer Burns advised me to put it in a fund for you, and you would be glad for it someday. I've been tempted to give it to you several times when the going was hard, but something kept me from it. Now, I know, is the proper time." She laid the small bankbook on the table in front of Nancy.

Nancy was dumbfounded. She opened the little book and looked at the neat figures entered from time to time as interest was figured over a period of twenty-six years.

"Someday the Lord might call Boyd to preach the gospel."


# CHAPTER 26

"Dear Mom and Dad," read Nancy. She read part of Boyd's letter sent from Marshall College, and then Steve waited on a cookie customer. She had to stop three times before she could finish reading the letter to Steve.

"Would you mind too much if I went to summer school? I want to take more Bible subjects. I feel as though I must get through and get into active service as soon as possible."

Steve sat on a stool. "If he's bound to go to college, he may as well work at it and get it over."

\* \* \*

Nancy's heart contracted when she looked at Steve's white wavy hair. He was more handsome at seventy than he had been at forty, she thought, but she noticed his steps were slower when he went to pick up the morning paper.

"May already," remarked Steve as he seated himself opposite Nancy at the breakfast table. "Seems like I reckon time from one harvest to another. I'm going to work in the harvest again this year."

Nancy's spoon halted midway to her mouth. This problem hadn't reared its ugly head for several years.

"You're too old."

Steve put back his head and laughed. "Not too old to do what I'm going to do."

"What are you going to do?"

"I'm going to weigh grain down at Fiester's grain elevator."

"You are?"

"Claude Fiester asked me if I would. All I have to do is sit on a stool in front of the scales all day. I told him I'd talk it over with you. Neither one of us is as spry as we once were, and harvest always brings more demand for baked goods."

"I—I guess I can manage."

"I'll get a dollar fifty an hour. Couldn't you get one of Bill's girls to help? You wouldn't have to pay her nearly that much."

Boyd's letters were a constant source of joy to Nancy. At last the harvest was over, and Steve was helping her to stir batters again.

"We ought to get one of those big mixers," he said as he rested for the sixth time from kneading the dough.

"Let me do it." She looked at him anxiously.

"There comes Henry Cameron. I want to talk to him." Steve hurried out as Henry's pickup drove to the front of the Buttercup Bakery.

Steve was gone only a short while. He came into the bakery. "Say, Nan, Henry wants company for a trip to Mason City. You don't mind if I go along, do you?"

Before Nancy could answer Steve hurried into the living room. "Get me a sandwich, so I won't have to spend money for lunch."

Annoyed, Nancy went to the cash register and took out two dollars. "Here," she said as she went toward the living-room door. "I'm too busy to make a sandwich. You can buy—"

"I told you to make me a sandwich," he shouted as Nancy saw him stuff something that looked like one of their bank deposit bags into his pocket. "Get on out there and do as I told you."

She backed away. She hadn't seen Steve so angry for a long time. Dropping the money on the counter, she retreated to the kitchen. The front door slammed.

*Henry's gotten impatient and come in to see what's keeping Steve,* she mused. She cut her finger slicing the ham.

"Here," Nancy was wrapping the sandwich as she hurried into the bakeshop. "Here's your sandwich." She looked about the room bewilderedly. The bakery was empty. Henry's pickup was gone.

Knead bread dough. Mix cookie dough. *Oh dear! My pies are getting too brown. There goes Mrs. Way's waitresses. It must be after three. I can hardly manage all this alone. I don't have time to run after one of Bill's girls. I need a telephone.*

*Four o'clock and I'm only loafing my bread.* She baked two batches of cookie orders while she waited for the bread to rise.

The kitchen clock struck seven times.

"Seven o'clock!" she said aloud, "No wonder I'm about ready to drop. I didn't even have lunch." Hastily she ate the sandwich that she had prepared for Steve and drank a glass of milk.

Nancy rested her head on the steering wheel of the delivery truck as it was parked by the back door of the Way-Side Café. As she pulled slowly onto Main Street, she noticed the clock inside the café said ten o'clock.

"Now to wash the dishes," she said to the empty bakeshop. The shades were lowered. The light above the sink made her shadow long and slim as she reached from counter to sink. From sink to counter. "Washing dishes at midnight. Where could Henry Cameron be keeping Steve this long. I didn't think Henry drank. There I go again . . . losing faith."

The knock on the front door made her jump.

"Whoever is there is impatient," remarked Nancy as the door shook under the insistent pounding.

"Who's there?" she called fearfully.

"Henry Cameron."

"Henry Cameron!" Her hands could hardly undo the lock quickly enough.

"I left that fool of a man of yours," he stormed angrily before he had stepped inside the door.

"You left Steve?" she looked inquiringly at Henry who looked as though he'd spent a night sleeping in his clothes.

"Yes, I left the—the—" He was too angry to go on. "He's in Mason City, and I don't care how he gets home."

"What's the matter?"

"I waited as long as I could, even longer. He got outa my pickup at eleven o'clock this morning. Said his business would take 'bout an hour, and I should pick 'im up at the Lunch Wagon. I waited till I couldn't anymore. I tramped the streets, drove up and down, and I couldn't find 'im. He can walk home for all I care, but I want my money."

"Money?" questioned Nancy.

"Yes, money," screeched the irate man. "I ain't 'bout to drive clear to Mason City and let my farm work wait fer nothin.'"

"But—but. . . ." She hardly knew what to say.

"Steve said he'd pay me six bucks if I took him to Mason City on business. When I come to pick 'im up, I had to wait on 'im. I took him and feel I earned my six bucks waitin' even if I didn't bring him home."

Stunned, Nancy went to the kitchen and got six dollars to pay Henry Cameron.

# CHAPTER 27

"I'm listening for that faltering footstep," Nancy told herself as she sat down to a solitary supper.

"If only I had faith." She laid her head on the table.

"Lord," she sobbed, "must I pay for my mistakes the rest of my life?" Minutes ticked by. Nancy's supper grew cold before the sobs subsided.

Morning brought sunshine and new hope. "I'll not look up the street when the Mason City bus comes in today," she resolved.

When the five o'clock bus from Mason City started from its stopping place a block west of their house, Nancy went on working.

"Kitty," Nancy told her sleek gray cat as she once more placed the remainder of her uneaten supper in the cat's dish. "You will get fat if

Steve—doesn't—come. . . ." She fled to her bedroom and wept and prayed until she slept.

Something had awakened her. Nancy lay rigid under the mended blue spread, listening. *There is the noise again. Someone is trying to get in the bakeshop door.*

Suddenly the night air was split by a clatter that brought Nancy to her feet. "Oh, Lord, what shall I do?" she unconsciously prayed. "Someone is trying to break the door down. Steve has a key. It can't be—"

Another clatter sent Nancy running to Boyd's bedroom to look out a front window.

*One! Two! Three!* The kitchen clock struck. A male voice mumbled below. Nancy trembled. She could see a large dark figure moving on the front step. Cautiously she raised the window and leaned out far enough so that she could see the front door.

The figure on her doorstep moved. *It's a big dog,* thought Nancy with relief. *No, it's a man kneeling trying to pick open the lock.*

She was stiff with fright. He was slowly pulling himself to a standing position. Was he going to break the door?

"Oh!" exclaimed Nancy aloud when the man fell over something at his feet and a clanking clatter accompanied the figure rolling down the two cement steps to the pavement. A cloud of profanity rose to strike Nancy the same time that the realization struck her that Steve had faltered home.

*　　*　　*

After two weeks of puttering, muttering, and going from one hardware store to another, Steve finally had the large mixer which he had brought from Mason City fixed.

Nancy wondered disgustedly how many times he had fallen with or on the stainless steel mixing bowls. She wondered also what had taken place in Mason City. Steve sat dejectedly whenever there wasn't any dough to mix.

Friday was the busiest day of the week. "There are two extra cakes to bake yet this evening. I'll help carry the pies to the truck and get to stirring up the cakes."

"Deliver your own pies," was Steve's curt answer.

"But, Steve, I have to get supper and bake two cakes."

"I might hit something with the truck," he grumbled as he went into the living room.

"I'll have to give Mrs. Way one less apple pie." Nancy put a warm apple pie on the kitchen table and set plates for two before she climbed wearily into the delivery truck.

When she returned, she hurried in the door.

"I'll just get the cakes in the oven to bake while we eat."

It took her only a half hour to get both batters into layer pans and into the oven.

"Steve." She went to the living-room door.

"Come on out to supper now. Steve!" He was gone.

She stopped short at the kitchen table. "Could one man eat a whole pie? The milk is all gone too." She shook her head sadly. "I can't understand what ails him. He hasn't been drinking since the Mason City episode. He just acts so strange."

She frosted the cakes and washed the pans and dishes.

"It looks like he's on a drinking spree now. Where else could he be at midnight?"

She worried through Saturday and was relieved when he came home early in the evening.

"What's in the package, Steve?"

Nancy knew better than to ask where he had been all night and all day, but he had never brought liquor into their home before. She was certain that the bottle showing above the paper sack contained nothing good.

He winked. "Something to make me forget." He laughed an unnatural laugh.

"Forget what, Steve?" Anxiety made her voice tremble.

"That I married you when I was young, but now I'm old."

"Steve, quit talking like that."

*     *     *

"Come on, Steve," urged Nancy the next morning. "Get up and go to church with me."

153

"Let me alone," came the muffled answer from the pillow.

"You'll feel better if you go."

"Let me be," shouted Steve as he sat up and then dropped down on the pillow again.

Her heart was heavy when she slid behind the wheel of the delivery truck and turned its nose toward church.

*He's never acted like this before.*

Elmer Burns seemed to have little difficulty in launching into the theme of his sermon. "The Need for Repentance" was a subject on which he could speak loud and long.

Several boys in the center of the church nudged each other. Their eyes wandered toward the road. Nancy saw the cloud of dust about the same time she heard the roar of the car engine. Gravel flew across the porch of the church as the car tore into the driveway. Even before the tires ground to a halt, feet were pounding across the porch.

"Fire! Fire!" The cry rose above Elmer's voice. Everyone was on their feet. "Bakeshop's on fire! Every man to the job!" The boy panted at the door before he turned and leaped into the already moving car that roared its way back to town.

"If they'd only move faster," cried Nancy as she ran toward her truck.

"Come on, Sis." Bill's voice was quiet as he propelled her to the side opposite the driver and he climbed behind the wheel. "Sally'll bring our car. She's organizing a prayer group among the women."

Dust swirled thick on the road as carload after carload of men raced toward town.

"Oh, Bill," sobbed Nancy. "Steve's not ready to die."

"He has sense enough to get out."

"He's—he's—there's something wrong with him. He brought a bottle of liquor home last night," she wailed.

"It can't be too bad. I don't see any smoke." Bill honked. The milling crowd moved a little.

The fire engine was throbbing in front of the house, but the front of the house looked all right.

"Let's leave the car." They were still a block away. Nancy raced around to the back of the house. She could see smoke coming from the rear of the house.

"The living room!" panted Nancy. The wall of the living room was charred up into their bedroom.

"Steve's in there!" screamed Nancy.

Bill held her tight to keep her from going inside.

"He's safe at Hopkins' next door." Nancy went limp and was carried next door also.

# CHAPTER 28

She sat facing Doctor Braddock in his office.

"Nancy, I don't know what to say. You have weathered so much with Steve."

"Why can't I go to see him, Doctor? You say he isn't badly burned."

"If you insist, I'll take you along to Sylvan Springs this afternoon, but—" he paused.

"But what?"

"It isn't the burns on Steve's hands that I'm concerned about. I had hoped Steve would snap out of this and I wouldn't have to tell you."

"Tell me what?" she sank back into the large chair.

"He's not quite—well—himself."

"What is 'himself,' Doctor Braddock? He has so many different 'selves.'"

"I may as well put it straight to you, Nancy. Steve has to be watched."

Her frightened eyes grew wider.

"I wish I wouldn't need to tell you, but I feel you must know. Steve is fortunate to be alive. Seth Hopkins saw—the fire in your living room was set, Nancy." The doctor groaned and hid his face.

"What are you trying to say?"

"Steve was drunk—there is no doubt about that. Seth and his wife observed him stagger to the garage. He took some newspaper and a can into the house. . . ."

"Are you implying that Steve set fire to our home?" She was angry.

"He probably didn't mean to set fire to the house, but drink had dulled his mind. He didn't realize. Hopkins heard the explosion. He ran over and his wife telephoned the fire department. If it were not for that, you wouldn't have a house left. Seth found Steve crouched under the counter in the bakeshop. This also saved him. Had he run after he was showered with the gas . . . . Let's try to forget that part."

"What about Steve?"

"He keeps babbling about something he wants to forget. It seems as though he was trying to destroy evidence or a reminder. I don't understand. Maybe his babblings mean nothing."

"What time do you leave for Sylvan Springs?"

"I'll leave at one-thirty."

"Don't leave without me."

Doctor Braddock got out of the car in front of the hospital.

"I want to see Steve alone first," said Nancy.

"I think it is a mistake, but I'll be right outside the door at the desk," the doctor replied.

*Of what is he afraid?* Nancy wondered as she knocked on the door and entered.

"Hello, Steve." She held her breath. He looked wild as he sat staring into space.

"I don't have it. It was in the desk. It's gone," he shouted wildly. "I knew you'd come to hound me."

"Steve! It's Nancy."

"She's come to hound me, and I won't tell. It burned. It's burned!" She turned to see to whom he was speaking. She hadn't heard the doctor and a nurse slip in the door.

157

*They think he's insane,* thought Nancy. Unafraid she took his bandaged hand between hers. "It's your Nan. Don't you know me?"

"You can't prove it. You can't," he muttered. She ran her hand through his white wavy hair.

"Did they wash your hair? It's as fine as silk."

"They washed it yesterday."

"Your hands are almost well, the doctor tells me." She continued to stroke his hair as she spoke of the bakery, the neighbors, and Bill's girls.

"Did you know Rhoda is engaged to a fine young minister?"

Steve didn't reply.

"I had a letter from Boyd today," she continued.

"Is he studying hard?" asked Steve.

"I believe so. The last year in college means a lot of hard work."

"Don't tell him. . . . I mean don't bother him with our troubles."

Boyd had already been told, but she refrained from saying this to Steve.

"I'll have to go now."

"Please come again, Nan."

"All right. Tomorrow."

Doctor Braddock called Nancy the next morning.

"Nancy, the hospital called this morning. Steve slept all night. He's so much better. I wish I had taken you sooner."

"He probably would not have been ready for my presence sooner."

158

*   *   *

"Nancy." Doctor Braddock spoke softly. The warm afternoon sun shone in the car. Two weeks of trips between Dry Forks and the hospital had passed.

She roused from her dozing.

"Did you speak to me?"

"I hate to wake you, but it seems necessary to talk some things over. We may as well do it on our long ride."

"Twenty-three miles shorten considerably when traveled every day."

"Especially when one sleeps the greater part of the trip. Nancy, you can't keep it up, working half the night so that you can visit Steve every afternoon."

"I know."

"He's all right, I guess. I asked Doctor Howe to check him. He's a specialist in the field." His voice was heavy with meaning.

The silence wore on as mile after mile of flat prairie moved by the car windows. Nancy swallowed all the questions she would have liked to ask.

"Is the house fixed?" asked the doctor at last.

"Yes."

"Then I'll bring him home tomorrow. But. . . ."

"But what?"

"He can't be allowed to be alone at all."

"I'll never leave him alone in the house again if I can help it. He was acting strange before this happened. I should have known there was something more than drink."

# CHAPTER 29

"What's keeping them so long," said Nancy as she went to the window for the tenth time to look for the doctor who was bringing Steve home.

Men from the church had volunteered to fix the burned portion of the house.

"Couldn't we just board up the back of the house?" Nancy had asked. "We can use Boyd's bedroom until he comes home—then we can decide what to do." She couldn't bring herself to tell Brother Burns or even her brother Bill that if Steve needed a great deal of care and watching, she couldn't keep on baking. But then what else would she do for a living?

A car door slammed out front. Nancy watched as Doctor Braddock helped Steve from the car. Steve looked old, and Nancy suddenly felt old.

"Come in. Come in." She held the door open for the two men to enter.

"Smells good in here," said Steve.

"Your wife is the best pie baker in town, Steve."

There seemed to be an uneasy air in the room.

"Come into the kitchen. I'll get a piece of pie and some coffee. You must be hungry after such a long drive."

Warm May sunshine lay in patches on the table but Nancy shivered. Something was not right. Doctor Braddock followed her into the kitchen.

"You're alone?"

"Mrs. Hopkins will come over and sleep on the couch tonight if you insist."

"I insist. He—"

"Nancy! Nancy!" Steve's cry was almost like that of an animal wild with pain.

The two in the kitchen ran to Steve in the bakery. He stood in front of the new wall where once was the door into the living room.

"The door! The door?"

"It burned, Steve. We fixed it this way for a while until you can fix it the way you want it."

They followed him out the back door as he ran to the place where the living room once stood.

"It's gone. I didn't just dream it. It's gone." His voice sounded funny. "My desk is gone too."

"Come indoors, Steve. Your desk is gone." Nancy led him like a small boy. He slumped into a chair. "It's really gone." He smiled an unnatural smile. "My papers are gone too."

Nancy went to the garage. She soon returned with a metal box. "Don't be upset, dear. You were smart. Your papers are probably unharmed if you have them in this metal box. I found it in the ashes." She set the metal box on the table before him.

"No!" he screamed. "Even fire didn't destroy it. You think you're clever. You found out at last.

161

You knew I couldn't beat you with burned hands."

"Steve," Nancy's voice was sharp and loud. "I did not touch your things."

Doctor looked at Nancy for an explanation.

"It's been an obsession of his through the years that someone is trying to take something of his that he kept locked in his desk."

"Go ahead and open it," he screamed. "I don't care. The devil's hounding my tracks. I don't care. Open it and let me be." He took the box, held it above his head, and hurled it against the stove with a mighty force.

"Steve!" whispered Nancy after the clanking of metal on metal had quit. The room was filled with an eerie quietness.

Steve put his head on the table. Great sobs shook his frame. All three seemed to avoid looking at the spilled contents of the box.

"What should we do?" Nancy was almost too frightened to speak.

"Steve," the doctor put his hand on his shoulder and spoke sternly. "Steve, what is it that you are hiding?"

"First Doctor Howe and now you." Steve sounded like an old man speaking. "Who told you?"

"Told me what, Steve."

"That—I—I—was married," sobbed Steve.

"Married?" said Nancy and the doctor in unison. "What do you mean?"

"Bring me the papers." He pointed to the

162

papers strewn across the floor.

"I have never touched your papers, and I won't now. I knew the desk was unlocked sometimes, and I never meddled with it." She put her hands behind her back.

"I will," said the doctor angrily as he started to gather up the papers. "Something that drives a man to act this way should be looked into."

"This is—my first—marriage certificate," sobbed Steve. "My wife and children."

Nancy could say nothing as she once more looked into the smiling eyes of the photograph of the woman and two children.

"My wife and boys—Steven and David."

The silence of the kitchen was broken by the striking of the clock.

"All these years you have lived a lie. I—you—words just fail when I think how Nancy has slaved and stuck by you."

"I know. I know." Fresh sobs shook him. "I have tried to be a Christian or pretend I was one, but that didn't work. I tried to drown it with drinking. I tried to destroy the evidence and myself with fire, but God wouldn't even allow that." His voice had risen to screaming again. "What can I do?"

"Nancy," said the doctor, "call your minister."

Mechanically she obeyed.

Doctor Braddock stayed with them until Elmer Burns and his wife came, and then he left them alone. Steve did not move. Nancy walked about restlessly.

"We came as soon as we could," said Mrs. Burns. "I helped Elmer finish choring."

Silence filled the corners of the small kitchen as darkness crept in.

"Let's pray together," said the minister.

"Kind Father, You know our needs before we ask. Be with Steve and Nancy. Heal the wounds. If we can help them in their trouble, direct us. Amen."

Steve started to speak:

"I ran away from a drunken father. At sixteen I married a girl twelve years older than I. She was from a drinking family too. We drank. We separated. Lived together again and drank and fought some more. I left before David was born. She sent me that photograph and begged me to come home." Steve's voice was almost inaudible. "I went home and saw David—but—but—" Steve cried so that he could no longer talk.

"If you'd rather not tell it, Steve," said Elmer Burns kindly, "it's between you and Nancy."

"I have to get it off my chest. It's driving me crazy."

Between sobs he spoke again. "David was a hopeless cripple. At a year when I last saw him he—he—couldn't even raise his head. She blamed it all on me. I joined a harvest crew and drifted. I never entered the state of Oklahoma again.

"When I met Nancy, she was the first Christian I ever knew. She attracted me. I meant to love her and leave her as I had done with women

164

in practically every town where the harvest crew stayed. She let down on her Christian principles to date me, but all others she held to. She should have never gone out with me. She has been faithful. . . ." The group in the kitchen waited while Steve again fought for control.

"I stole." His voice sounded like a shout in the quiet. "I took the money Nancy earned with her hands and went to Mason City or pretended to go there and went elsewhere and sent money to her so she wouldn't try to make me come home. I made sure no one would trace me.

"I never heard from Inez again. My son Steve would be thirty-eight years old, and if David is living, he is thirty-six."

"I took Nancy's money and some from Boyd," he cried.

Steve rose. "Here in this metal box is the evidence. God wouldn't allow me to destroy it."

Nancy sat in a daze, stunned as the awful truth struck her. *Not only has Steve deliberately deceived me, but all these years I have been living in adultery,* she thought.

Aloud Nancy repeated Galatians 6:7, "Be not deceived; God is not mocked: for whatsoever a man soweth, that shall he also reap. I am only reaping what I have sown."

Steve ranted and raved, no longer coherent.

At length Elmer Burns rose and faced Nancy. "Under the circumstances we will take Steve home with us."

Nancy was glad for the decision. Already the

doctor had warned that she should not stay with him alone, and she also knew she could no longer live with this man.

She was not surprised when a few days later Boyd returned home to help care for his father.

# CHAPTER 30

Nancy paused and listened. A familiar whir and chug reached her ears. The June sunlight cast glimpses of color like that of ripened wheat among the wisps of her whitening hair. She looked out across the fields at the combine just starting to cut Elmer Burns' wheat. When the wheat was cut she would again be able to see the Burns' house where Boyd and his family also lived. Slowly she lowered her thin work-stiffened knees to the patch of oak-leaf lettuce and cut a panful.

Thoughtfully she walked toward the house she now shared with her brother and his family. Only two of the nine girls were at home anymore.

Nancy knocked on the door of her brother's side of the house before entering.

"I have cut the first lettuce," she called as she set the pan on the sink and started to leave. "I'll just leave it here for your supper."

"Thank you," called Sally from deep within the house. "Bill and the girls have some business to take care of before they come home tonight so supper will be quite late." Sally spoke as she came through the house to the kitchen.

"You are coming over to share supper with us, aren't you?"

"I guess I will since you are so kind to invite me," replied Nancy as she was leaving. She paused at the door. "Since they will be late anyway, I think I'll just walk out and watch the combine a bit."

"Have they started combining?" asked Sally. "I hadn't noticed. I was upstairs putting some clothes away."

Slowly Nancy walked past the few houses that edged the town. Thoughts crowded in. So many years it seemed and so many times she had trod this road she was taking. Hardly realizing where her steps were taking her, she moved toward the small church out beyond the town limits. She was being drawn to the church, the graveyard, and memories.

Nancy lifted her eyes as the large combine came into view. But it was soon far away and only a faint hum accompanied her memories. Tears fell as she looked at the stones bearing the names of her parents. She was only a child when Father had died, and Mother was gone almost five years now. The small stone indicating the place her tiny baby girl was laid, brought more tears. She had never even held her in her arms.

"I'm sure my baby is with Jesus. But—"Nancy sobbed as her eyes sought the stone with Steve's name on it.

Memories flooded in upon her. She thought of the years of hardship she had shared with the man who never was and never could have been her legal husband. According to the Word of God she had lived in sin all those years.

*Yes,* she thought, *I know I am forgiven, but that will never change the past. All those wasted years.*

More tears flowed as she thought of all the years Boyd had spent helping Elmer Burns care for Steve in his agitated state of mind. Then the time had come when Steve had needed more care and restraint than Elmer Burns, Boyd, or all the congregation could give, so that he had spent his final wretched months in a mental institution.

She was glad Boyd had stayed on helping Elmer Burns who was getting older and when Boyd married he had gone into partnership with the aged minister.

Nancy lifted her tear-swollen eyes and viewed the fields of the Burns farm. They were having a bountiful harvest.

"Be not deceived," Nancy reproached herself, "God is not mocked, for whatsoever a man soweth, that shall he also reap."

"If only I had listened," she lamented. "I could have been spared such a bitter harvest of tears."